Reading A Writer's Mind
**Exploring Short Fiction –
First Thought to Finished Story**

...you'll find advice on character forming and building, plot structure, language choice, viewpoint selection and much more...

...her thinking on characterisation is especially enlightening...

...a great help. I would recommend it to anyone wanting to write...

This is the first in the
Reading A Writer's Mind
series of writers' guides

Further information can be found at
http://lindaacaster.blogspot.com
http://www.lindaacaster.com

Reading A Writer's Mind

Exploring Short Fiction First Thought To Finished Story

Linda Acaster

Linda Acaster

Reading A Writer's Mind
Exploring Short Fiction –
First Thought to Finished Story

First Edition paperback
This edition copyright © 2013 Linda Acaster
ISBN: 978-1484179734

All stories highlighted in this work are the
copyright of Linda Acaster. Individually they have been
published in various UK and international magazines
and anthologies over a number of years.
Each is a work of fiction. Names, characters, places and
incidents are either the product of the author's imagination
or are used fictitiously.

Also available as an ebook in Kindle and ePub formats
© 2011 Linda Acaster

All rights reserved.
No part of this publication may be reproduced or
transmitted in any form without the express written
permission of the author. This book is protected under
the copyright laws of the United States of America.
Linda Acaster also asserts the moral right to be
identified as the author of this work under the
UK Copyright, Designs and Patents Act 1988.

About the Author

Linda Acaster began her writing career concentrating on short fiction before moving to novels and non-fiction articles. Along the way she started teaching adults the art and craft of creative writing, and by accident laid bare the mechanics of her thought processes. Using her own short fiction as dissecting models, she shares some of the ways she distils her craft in *Reading A Writer's Mind: Exploring Short Fiction – First Thought to Finished Story*.

> 'When creating fiction, many professional writers make decisions on their craft because of a gut-feeling that it is right for that particular scene on that particular occasion. As a teaching tool, such ethereal reasoning is useless to someone trying to hone their skills. My aim is to be detailed in my explanations, using language and concepts that can be understood by both the new and the more experienced writer of short fiction.'

Linda Acaster has been a reader for a leading London literary consultancy and a tutor with a UK distance learning college. She has over 70 published short stories to her credit, five novels, and numerous instructional articles on the techniques of creating fiction.

About the Book

Ever read narrative fiction and wondered how the author came to produce it?

Reading a Writer's Mind: Exploring Short Fiction – First Thought to Finished Story shows the detailed thinking behind ten stories across a range of genres using differing forms of delivery. From the introductory aims of each narrative, through the story itself, to a commentary explaining the decisions made during the writing, *Reading a Writer's Mind* offers a unique insight into one writer's creative process, laying a path to follow and showing the tools to use.

Whether you are a reader interested in the mechanics of story production, or a new writer wrestling with the technicalities of bringing your vision to paper for others, there is much to be gained from this absorbing guide.

Contents

About the Author v

About the Book vi

Shared With The Light 11
Mainstream, 4,200 words.
Present tense, first person male viewpoint.
How to build a story from a character. Lyrical narrative versus terse dialogue. Using Tone as a descriptive tool. The importance of interrogating the initial idea.

Contribution To Mankind 33
Horror, 3,700 words.
Past tense, first person male viewpoint.
Toning in the dark side of human nature: characterisation through deed and thought. Describing without description. The importance of a plausible back-story.

What Constitutes Women's Fiction? 53
An introduction to the next four stories, dispelling popular misconceptions.

Permanently Portugal 55
Mainstream, 1,200 words.
Past tense, selected omniscient viewpoint.
A Tell story using a calendar structure. Being intentionally heavy on narrative. Using distance between the story and the reader as a cloaking device. The importance of naming.

An Interesting Day In The Office   67
Women's Fiction, 2,500 words.
Past tense, first person female viewpoint.
Keeping the reader guessing to ensure a twist-in-the-tale story doesn't disintegrate into a tale-of-the-painfully-obvious. Gathering story elements into a workable idea. The importance of pacing.

Turning Back The Clock   83
Women's magazine fiction, 2,900 words.
Past tense, first person female viewpoint.
Drip-feeding back-story to add tension and promote anticipation. The use of alliteration, rhythm and subliminal detailing to bolster the romance. The importance of market study.

Jeremy   97
Women's magazine fiction, 4,100 words.
Past tense, third person male viewpoint.
An *ahh* story. A cross-generational storyline using the eternal triangle to emotionally lift the characters and the reader. Producing fiction from a theme. Choosing characters. When it is useful to add back-story at the front. The importance of using 'show' rather than 'tell' to wring an emotional response from the reader.

A Bird In The Hand   117
Crime, 4,000 words.
Past tense, first person male viewpoint.
Building a story from a given line. Using an unsympathetic character to carry a story without the aid of name or description. Motive from character. Manipulating a reader's reaction. The importance of planning characters.

Harvester World TZ29-4   137
Science Fiction, 4,100 words.
Past and present tense, first person female viewpoint.
Using a parallel storyline structure to convey the current story and a back-story. Techniques used to create a society different from, but recognisable to, our own. The importance of reader anchorage points.

Doppelganger   159
Fantasy, 4,450 words.
Past tense, first person male viewpoint.
Making the everyday fantastical by preying on the insecurities of the main character, and by default, the reader. The importance of structure.

A Wind Across The Plains   181
Historical, 700 words.
Present tense, first person female viewpoint.
Writing for performance and sound effects. When prose becomes poetic through the use of rhythm and repetition. The importance of structure.

Editing   189
Ten common problems that cause a story to fall short of its potential. The importance of being professional.

Other Titles by Linda Acaster   195

An Introduction To

Shared With The Light

Many new writers begin to improve their skills levels by attending Adult Education classes, and this is where *Shared With The Light* was born.

As the group's tutor, I was giving pointers on how to build characters from scratch rather than writing about someone students knew. Real people we learn to understand from the outside in, usually from years of close proximity where we witness their reactions to external forces and gradually gain a better view of what makes them tick. Fictional characters we need to understand from the inside out so that their written reactions to what happens round them is based on what makes them tick. To break it down to a sound-bite: with a real person we see the effect and try to understand the cause; with a fictional character we need to understand the cause to be able to write the realistic effect.

For ease, I asked the group to contemplate one character. I was determined to make this character genderless so that members of the group could make their own decisions on this person without being influenced by me or by pressure from the group. I asked for suggestions as to likely occupations of people we might see working on the street. A list was drawn up and a vote taken. The character everyone would write about was to be a busker.

Then I threw in a *What if..?* What if someone approached to speak to the busker? Who would it be, and why? Members of the group had a week to come up with an answer.

Of course, not all Adult Education groups are passive. Mine was adamant. If members were being asked to produce a short story using this premise, they wanted to see my version. So here it is.

Shared With The Light

I don't know why I picked this tune. I play it sometimes for practice, for a memory of the old times when the walls crowd in and I begin to yearn for the sharp taste of a beer, but I never play it to an audience, not this audience at least. They're not real; not feeling, thinking beings who can offer a smile or an acknowledgement of talent that is there. Or was there, once. They're as lost as I am. At least I have this tune. They, probably, have nothing.

I draw the sax into my body, hugging it like a slender lover. Filling my lungs for the final phrase, I move towards the climax, finishing the run on a long note squeezed between drying lips and the quavering reed. Perspiration stands on my skin, beading across the small of my back as the muscles strain. Like the old times there is a tingling in thigh and shoulder, and I cradle the sax as if it is made from filigree glass. But it isn't the same with my eyes open, even with them slit. It isn't a tune to be shared with the light.

Disappointment grows as the note fades. There will be no emerging from exquisite ecstasy, only the familiar dragging from the depths of despair.

I'm not sure if it is the uncertain applause that snaps me back or the chinking of the coins as one falls upon another. Fifty pence pieces are distinctive, and this is different. The sound of pound coins reverberates like small arms fire in the domed arcade, and I raise my arms expansively to smile and take a bow, the theatre of playing an audience kicking in automatically. They stand before me, clutching tight their festive gifts, dripping rain into bright puddles on the checkerboard of polished tiles.

'That were great.'

'Thank you,' I say, sweeping my gaze across the smiling faces, wanting none to miss the appreciation I'm broadcasting.

'—thank you, thank you—', but the moment is already passing. They're shuffling away, embarrassed at listening, embarrassed at being touched.

'That were great.'

I swing round to the voice. He is younger than me, half a lifetime younger, gingery stubble patched uncertainly on his throat and lower cheeks, but I know the eyes. As bright as cut diamonds. As piercing as the knife he undoubtedly carries in a back pocket.

He takes a step towards me oblivious to those he cuts across, grey people in their grey world now oblivious to me in mine. His step lengthens into two, and I feel my every muscle tense.

'That were absolutely fan-tastic.'

I don't recognise the accent; try to memorise him – his blue eyes, his taller height, his limp fair hair – so that I'll recognise the mugshot, but my brain doesn't want to take it in. His lips part in a grin and the familiar smell of strong mints overwhelms me.

'You were really lost in that one. You were brilliant.'

I wish he would go, know that he won't. It's my move.

'Thank you,' I say.

His gaze begins to drop, and the remnants of my soul drop with it. We stand together, our toes separated by the thin line of the sax's case, its red plush interior marbled with bronze and silver and gold. He is counting. I know in the flick of a practised eye. Enough to eat for a week. Not enough to get knifed for.

'Good pitch, eh?'

'The rain,' I say. 'It drives them inside. Luck.'

I glance at his feet, at the white trainers with the blue bindings, at the lack of water puddled round them. He will know about the coins I've tucked into my pocket. He's been watching me that long, at least.

'D'ya read?'

My gaze flicks back to his face, to the arrogant openness of youth.

'Read?'

'Is it by ear, or d'ya read the music?'

He's left it too long, lost his bottle.

'Both,' I say.

'That one?'

'Long ago. I can't remember.'

His gaze moves to the sax and I tighten my grip on it. Only once has it been wrenched from my grasp, and I was lucky that time. I won't be lucky here. I feel the dent beneath my palm, smooth the lasting blemish as if it might lift through the heat of my hand.

'Alto, right?'

'Right,' I say.

'Not usual, that, is it?'

''tis for me.'

'I mean for that kinda tune. I 'eard a tenor tackle that one, but not as good as you.'

'Where did you hear this tenor?'

'Oh, years ago. It were a record me Dad 'ad. Used to play along.' He laughs. 'Sorta. The neighbours complained like crazy. That's 'ow I got sent to lessons.'

The truth begins to filter through. 'You play.'

I watch him cock his head. A couple of years ago I guess he would have blushed.

'Well, they all wants to play guitar, don't they? Like fleas on a dog. But a sax, well... The record gave it life, but you made it soar.'

I look at him and he at me. I'm not sure what I'm feeling, and can read even less in his youthful face.

'Your audience is waiting. Gonna play another?'

I have an audience of one. The rest is a flowing mass. 'Any requests?'

He grins again, looking more the excited boy. 'D'ya know *What's My Name?*'

I smile and wet my lips, placing the reed comfortably between my teeth. I was born knowing *What's My Name?*

He steps back to lean on a shop window, and it is only now that I remember the pound coins sitting at my feet, but it is too late. I'm pumped and primed and the notes are ringing in my head on their way down the tube to the bell.

I garner maybe two-fifty from it. The youth seems impressed. He comes to stand over me as I fish the big coins from the case.

'Never busked, meself. Lucrative?'

'Not so you'd notice. Do you gig?'

'Yeah. It's that I wanna talk t'ya about. D'ya fancy joining us? Meet the others an' 'ave a jam?'

I look into his face to see if he is pulling me along. I can no more read his thoughts than I could before, but he can obviously read mine.

'On the level, like. Honest.'

I laugh. 'Oh, sure.'

'Oh, sure what? You ain't 'eard us. You don't know 'ow good we are.'

'I know how old you are.'

'We're a mixed group. A quintet. Gary's twenty-eight. That can't be much younger than you.'

It isn't. 'I can't even remember being twenty-eight,' I say.

'Bullshit!'

I don't lie. Lies get a person nowhere but in a hole. 'What do you play?'

'Jazz. Blues. Some big band.'

'*Big band?*'

'You can get a lotta noise from a five-piece. You get a lotta noise from a one-piece.'

I don't deny him that. 'Two tunes and you are asking a busker to join your band? You must be a pretty desperate assortment.'

'We're a good assortment. Why don't ya come and listen?' His hand curves round to a pocket at the back of his jeans, and the unexpected movement chills me to the bone. When he produces a photocopied handbill I take it out of sheer relief.

'We're on at eleven. Not first act, you'll notice, so management of *Red Duster* can't think we're that desperate. Bring yer sax or leave it be, there'll be a ticket on't door f'ya.'

'You don't know my name,' I tell him.

'Marl Kerran,' he answers, and he leaves me to the grey mass shuffling through the arcade.

I push the key in the outer door and out of habit put my shoulder to the swollen wood. It screeches its welcome note and I cross the threshold into the dimly lit interior. Late night shopping is a killer, but there is no ignoring it. The week after Christmas takings will dive like a suicide from a bridge.

I drag myself and my packages up the uncarpeted stairway wrinkling my nose at the familiar smell. It is always worse after rain. The man from the pest control said it was the age of the house, the age of the plumbing. I'm sure it's a dead rat somewhere.

A child is crying, its noise drifting in and out of focus each time I turn a landing. It sounds oddly like a siren, and then I realise I'm hearing that, too, permeating the bricks like the rain and the stench of dead rat.

The flat is so cold my breath stands white before my lips. It didn't do that outside, I'd swear to anyone. Perhaps it did and I just didn't notice. I slip out of the raincoat and hang it behind the door to continue its quiet dripping onto the scuffed floorboards before switching on both bars of the fire and emptying the carrier. Two tins of lamb hotpot, teabags, dried milk, a small loaf. The usual fare.

With the contents of a tin fizzing in a pan, I go through the nightly routine of cleaning my sax. It is only when I'm nestling it back into its crimson lining that I notice the folded handbill the youth pressed on me. I read it while I stir my meal.

** For One Week Only **
The Mickey Lyons Quintet
Plays
The World Renowned RED DUSTER

I smile at the pretension, and wonder if that is his name, Mickey Lyons. It doesn't ring any bells. Neither the club, the *Red Duster*, world renowned or not, but its address makes me draw breath. Bridgewater Place, North Causeway. It's the *Tin Pan Alley* in another guise.

A door opens onto a memory so clear it could be a heartbeat away. Skeins of tobacco smoke curl through the crisp light of spotlamps, filling my nose, catching my throat. The clink of glasses, the scuffing of chairs, the low babble of voices lost in a darkness peppered with dull red lamps and the sharp yellow flaring of cigarette lighters. A silk shirt bonded, like a second skin, with sweat. And the whole lost to the tune, to my solo, to—

A crescendo shakes the ceiling, but it isn't mine. Johnson has been away for three days and now the blissful peace has ended. His music, his rave, fills the hollow above my room and floods down to engulf me. A child cries louder. A door on the landing below crashes back on its hinges. A woman shrieks abuse. Heavy footsteps race past and there is hammering on the door above. A man shouts violence in stark bass tones. The child cries louder. The woman shrieks. Hardcore rave sears through my veins like an overdose, and it is all I can do to reach for the bread and dip a slice into the part-heated stew.

The rain has stopped, but the crystal cold grips the damp raincoat and makes me shiver. I'm at the bottom of the street before the rave slips from my hearing, into the neon-puddled thoroughfare before it leaves my head.

The smell of fish and chips and curry runs fingertips over my taste-buds, and I hunch into my collar and cross between the buses to get away from it. Music pours between two black-suited guards on the door of a pub. Heavy rock from a jukebox. Laughter. Warmth.

I haven't brought the sax, wasn't intending to go to Bridgewater Place, but I'm heading that way, and what will it hurt to see the old facade again?

I remember the gutter, still full of water, but the cobblestones throw me. The entrance to the *Tin Pan Alley* had been down the passage between the old warehouses, but the *Red Duster* welcomes its clientèle on its main approach, up steps and through gaping double doors wide enough to take a small truck. *Bond House 17* is stencilled in glaring white on the bricks below the first floor windows. I don't recall that, either, but it looks new, at least repainted.

With my hands driven deep inside my raincoat pockets I hang back in the shadow of a nearby building. No one goes in. No one comes out. No one in black stands conspicuously at the door. There is nothing to smell but the decaying damp; nothing to hear but the distant drone of traffic and the occasional sing-song of sirens.

I walk up to the steps but don't climb, turning, instead, down the alley. A stark security light shines from high on the far wall casting spider-like shadows. There are boxes and overflowing waste bins on wheels. Behind them, wisps of steam rise in the chill of the night.

Lengthening my pace, I can feel my excitement quicken. The grille is still there, at the bottom of the wall. The same tapping fan throws out the smell of stale beer and cigarette smoke, but drifting on the warm air is the music. Faint, so very faint. I lean my hands against the cold bricks and turn my head to catch the sounds. A big bass, thrumming gently. A piano, yes, tinkling on the high notes. A guitar? Perhaps. It's difficult to tell. And then the sound of a sax bursts through. My gut turns. *Perdido*. I ache to be there, to be with them.

'Hey! You!'

I move quickly. Bouncers can be like lightning; hit first, ask questions later. The boots are steel-capped, the trousers loose, the coat dark, stained, half its buttons missing. Thin straggling hair creeps from beneath a blue wool skullcap to touch patched jowls part-hidden by an upturned collar. I blink at him and see consternation in his red-rimmed eyes, watch a thread of spittle creep over pasty lips.

His bearing changes. A finger rises to meet a nod of his head. His smile is wide, benign, all theatre.

'Sorry, guv. The ol' eyes, y'know. Not good in this light. Got a quid, like, for a man lost 'is way?'

Is that what he'd seen? Another alckie on his patch? Is that what I look like?

I give him a couple of coins and leave him to sort the bottle bins for the dregs of his life.

The weather has turned crisp by the morning, frost still clinging in shadowy nooks on the roof opposite when I pull back the curtain. The sunlight is dazzling, the sky as blue as the Med. The punters will be out from their offices during lunch. I've got to move if I'm to catch them. The motivation is easy enough. I've no tokens for the meter.

They are here in their scarves and their gloves, clutching their bright plastic carriers, but they're moving fast, their eyes on the windows, their minds on the time.

I trip like an amateur, miss four notes and fluff a run. I don't feel all here; hope to God it's not some virus. I collect three-eighty and consider myself fortunate.

I take myself into the cafe at the end of the arcade and sit in a corner with a bowl of soup, a cheese roll and half a pint of steaming tea. I'd be able to pay for a plated meal if I'd not given the wino so much, but the soup is warming and thick, and I try not to begrudge him the comfort.

My reflection bobs and spoons in the mirrored wall beside

me. I try to ignore it, but it beckons and waves, and in the end it has to be faced like so much has been faced in the past. I'm still thin. I haven't replaced the weight. I missed a patch on my neck, too, when I shaved, not much, but it stands like a dark signal against my skin. Pasty. Like the wino's.

I see the youth standing there, a reflection by the door, the blue eyes piercing, as bright as cut diamonds. I push away the empty bowl and start to undo the roll. He's at my table in a moment, blocking out the artificial daylight. He doesn't ask, just pulls the chair and sits.

'You didn't come.'

'No.'

'Why not?'

It isn't a polite question. He'd told them I would.

'Busy.' I take the knife and cut the roll.

He looks down, places his fingers on the edge of the table, careful not to encroach my space.

'Look, I know the *Red Duster* ain't top rank.'

'The *Duster's* fine.'

He looks up at me, surprised I'd interrupted. I hold his gaze.

'Audience, is there?'

'Yeah,' he says. 'Full last night.'

'Appreciative, are they?'

A smile creeps across his lips, the memory so close I can taste it. 'Yeah. Great.'

'Management pays up, does it? In full? On time?'

He gasps a single chuckle and nods like an amused two year old. I open my hands and grin at him, huge, benign, all theatre.

'Then you're fine.'

I watch his smile fade, his lips draw tight. From inside his jacket he brings a rectangular card and places it on the table between us. The words *Red Duster* stand bright and accusing in the centre.

'We can't do justice to *Autumn Leaves* wi'just one sax.' He holds me with those diamond eyes. 'It's our last night. I hope you ain't gonna be busy.'

Autumn Leaves goes down well with the shoppers, despite only one sax, despite it being an alto and not a tenor. I play it once during the afternoon and twice to the late-nighters. Brings me six pounds all on its own.

The notes of that tune ring in my head during the long walk home, right into the street where the cars crowd the gutter and reflect the weak lamplight, right up to the point where the hardcore rave breaks in.

I slow as I enter its periphery, hoping, praying, that the clear night air is carrying it from further up the street, that a distant window is open and an early party in progress. It's too much to ask.

Dragging leaden feet along the path, I fumble for the keys. The hammering, the crying child, the shrieking woman. It is as if the night has never turned. The uncarpeted stairs reverberate beneath my feet, the walls against my fingertips. I turn the landing clutching the sax case to my chest, trying to regain the peaks and lows of the duet. Hardcore rave pummels my brain, interferes with the rhythms, alters the notes. The man from downstairs is kicking Johnson's door, hammering the panels with God-knows-what. I don't want to know, don't want to see, don't want to hear, but it's impossible. I let myself into the flat and snap down the light switch. I'd forgotten. There are no tokens for the meter.

I lay beneath the blankets, cradling the soft lines of the sax in my arms, watching blue lights chase round the ceiling. There is no siren, though I hear it in my head. They come up the stairs all voices and boots, pass my door, the man shouting abuse, the woman shrieking. The child mewls unnoticed in the background, a distorted harmony. A call, another call, and the hammering starts again. Down the walls like sickly treacle, through the cold and lifeless air, pours the suffocating rave that calls itself music. It flattens me to the bed. It's flattening me into insanity.

And then the blankets are gone and the sax is nestling in its case. The door is slammed, the flashing lights passed, and I am striding along the street, the wall of sound subsiding behind the armour of my raincoat. By the time I make the thoroughfare my head is lifting, my senses, too, and the trilling notes of *Autumn Leaves* are pulsing through my blood.

I rush the steps to the double doors of Bond House 17, rush them in case I falter and turn back.

Reception is blinding bright, the walls covered in posters of acts classic before I was born. Matt black doors beckon into the inner sanctum, the lazy strains of *Weaver of Dreams* tantalizing my ears.

The woman behind the counter asks for my membership and I proffer the ticket. She looks at it in surprise, looks at me and squints.

'Marl Kerran?'

I blink back at her and nod.

'Mr Kerran,' she enthuses, the smile broad and genuine. 'I didn't recognise you. Hey, it's great to see you again. I hope it's not just a one-nighter.'

I smile as she gabbles. Should I know her? Was she here during the days of the *Tin Pan Alley*?

'Just let me call Rosalind and I'll take you side-stage. Can I relieve you of your coat?'

I don't want her to take my raincoat, to see my jacket or the unwashed shirt beneath. I wish I'd had some tokens for light to see to shave. I wish I hadn't come.

Rosalind arrives, a waft of sweet restrain flowing in her wake. Then I am through those sombre doors into a world of smoky darkness and the crisp cut of spotlights, the smell of beer and perfume and aftershave, the hubbub of voices, the clink of glassware. And out of the darkness grows the greyness of figures, the yellow and blue flash of cigarette lighters, the golden flicker of candle-glasses on tables. And the tone, the tone so sweet and perfect of the tenor sax. I don't want to move, don't want to breathe in case I spoil it.

The fair-haired youth stands centre stage in the dazzling light, his eyes shut, the tube cradled close as he runs the last notes to the end of the sequence. The audience applauds. The light widens for the others to take a bow: bass, piano, drums, a clarinet. The noise is thunderous, the clapping, the calls for more.

They're good.

I can't do it. Suddenly I can't do it, but the woman takes my arm and pulls me on, and despite my protests my feet carry me towards the stage. I don't want her to draw their attention but she's waving, and then he sees me. He's beside me, they're all beside me, shaking hands, offering names. And their warmth floods through me, lifting and sighing, bringing me home.

Let's do one now, they say, *do one now*.

I shed the raincoat, sloughing it like an unwanted skin. The blood begins pumping, the adrenalin high, and I'm called into the spotlight, the crisp white searing spotlight, to a roll of the drums and a round of applause.

What's My Name? hits them in the heart and me in the gut. There's no comparison to playing it in the arcade. It's another world, I another being.

We storm them with *Again 'n' Again*, and neither the floor nor the band will let me leave.

'I'm parched!' I cry above the din. 'I'm not used to this!' And a glass of bitter is pressed into my hand.

It is cold to my grasp, cold like the rime in the gutter of the cobblestoned alley. I gaze at the off-white head lapping the rim, and my throat constricts. I glance at the youth with the piercing eyes, his head thrown back, downing his like a man. What am I? What will I become? A shambling figure in a half-fastened coat weaving his way down an alley? Not with one. Surely not with just the taste of one.

It is sharp on my tongue, like a knife, but exquisitely teasing as it coats my throat, a sliver of fiery ice passing through my chest.

The floor is clapping in unison, chanting for more. The band have downed theirs and are retaking their places. The ivories tinkle a merry salute, the bass runs up an octave and down again, an athlete limbering up. And without a word being passed they are into *Autumn Leaves*.

Standing on the edge of the light, I let the tenor take the lead. I see the puzzled look, the frown cutting beneath limp, fair hair, but it's his band, his gig. All I want is to be a part of it again, a part of the music, a part of the moment that can be held like a bird and released. And so I stand in the shadow and close my eyes on the world, let the alto answer the tenor, court it and dance it and drive it and tantalise, always tantalise, the sax warm to my touch, responding like a lover, until all the notes have bloomed and faded and died.

I peel my lips from the reed and draw a lungful of smoky air, down, deep down, like the breath of gods. The floor erupts. Chairs screech back to hoots and whistles, and I open my eyes to the glaring white of the spotlight centred on me. I put out a hand, fending it away, turn to look for the tenor in my blindness. He is there, right beside me, pressing a glass into my hand.

'Fan-tastic! Fan-bloody-tastic! Drink up. We're gonna finish on your solo.'

And I drink from the poisoned chalice, a devotee sacrificing his life for the gifts of Heaven. A tingling in thigh and in shoulder. For a tune to be shared no more with the light, I give my life. Again.

Commentary

If the Adult Education group picked a busker, why did I pick a saxophonist? Because a colleague of my husband's played a saxophone in his spare time, which is true, but not notable enough to fix itself in my subconscious as possible writing material. I knew this man 'in passing' as shy and unassuming. Seeing him play in a pub was a revelation. With eyes closed he began making love to his saxophone from the very first note, and he had no idea that he was doing it. *That* is notable writing material.

Having a piece of notable writing material lodged in my subconscious does not immediately lead to a story, even when dredged up some months later by the requirements of a group exercise. Questions needed to be asked and decisions made. Time to call upon the writer's chattering friends: *who*, *what*, *where*, *when*, *how* and *why*.

Why decide my busker should be male? The real-life saxophonist was male, but I'm female. Isn't the given wisdom to write about what you know? I wanted the character to be vulnerable, at some sort of turning point in life. Vulnerable females are ten-a-penny. A vulnerable male holds more intrigue for me as a writer, probably because I'm female.

Why was he busking? Busking on the way up a musician's career is fairly normal, so I decided he was busking on the way down, or was at the nadir attempting to get his life back together.

What had happened to him to cause this? Pass. At this point I'd no idea.

Where was he busking? Somewhere warm, yet I wanted the weather to be bleak to resonate with his mindset. In the city near where I live, close to a modern shopping mall, is a late 19th century domed arcade. The difference in the acoustics of the two venues is spectacular and, as the story is about a musician, I chose the better acoustics. I decided it would be raining, hence pushing shoppers into the arcade, but why would he be there on a wet day, why would they be shopping on a wet day? Because it was the countdown to Christmas – the **when**. And that was the setting of the opening scene decided.

What type of music was he playing? A saxophone is not a normal instrument for a modern boy band, it is an instrument of a session musician, but I didn't want the character to be an also-ran, I wanted him to be a fallen star. It is here I should mention that what I know about music, or the playing of any instrument, can be written large on the reverse of a postage stamp. Not so much write about what you know as write about what can be learned. Time for a bit of research.

A query about saxophonists to a record-listening associate pointed me towards jazz, and a comb of the jazz CDs in the library not only established that saxophone solos were a recognised part of the form, but that there were different types of saxophones. Those CD jackets also provided music titles, and listening to those CDs provided tonal background – which tunes were jumping, which were lazy, which were duos. A book in the children's section named the parts of the instrument and explained how it was played. I could run with this research. My character was definitely playing jazz.

So who was he? I didn't want him to have been an international recording star, but I wanted him to have been far enough up the scale to be recognised and his talent acknowledged by an aficionado – and it was at this point that the person who would speak to him stepped into my mind. I knew that he – another he – was an aficionado, someone who had been brought up on the music and was also a musician, but in a lesser way – a younger self.

Teasing out the facets of a leading character and the main

thread of a storyline is often this step-by-step tapping at the coalface with a bent spoon – it can take hours, or days, or weeks – and then, miraculously, perhaps inspirationally, the face is tapped as before but this time the coal not only crumbles, it packs itself into containers, lifts itself to the surface, finds its own customer and delivers a profit, all in the taking of a single breath. In that breath I knew, just knew, that the younger self would be playing in a venue that had been a favoured spot of the lead character, that they both lived only for the music, that they would be sharing the same problem except that the younger self would be barely aware of it – alcoholism (note the early line ... *the familiar smell of strong mints overwhelms me*) – that the chain of events the meeting triggers would lead to a life or death decision by the lead character. And I knew which he would choose.

Having all the facets of the storyline unfold at once did not mean that the story as read unfolded at the same pace. There were other decisions to be made, starting with Viewpoint.

First person viewpoint was chosen because I wanted to get under the skin of the main character. I wanted to feel his every worry, see others as he would see them. I wanted him to have suffered so much in his recent life that he was not only alone, but distrusted others to the point of paranoia.

The choice of Tone aided this. I wanted his outer world to be depressing so as to feed his poor self image, the two acting one upon the other in a vicious circle. Tone comes across in the choice of words and phrasing. Taken singly the reader could step over each without conscious thought, but by loading certain paragraphs with negative images the tone becomes unremitting: *dimly* lit...late night shopping is a *killer*...takings will *dive* like a *suicide from a bridge*...the man from *pest control*...*dead rat* somewhere...

For the character, the one thing that was safe, that was comforting, that he could rely on, was his music. It is his reliance upon his music to the exclusion of all else that determines his thought patterns, and thus the technical use of symbolism and alliteration that I, as the writer, use to bring those thought patterns to an acceptable reality for the reader. His dialogue might be short and terse, but he notices the little things – *the white trainers with the blue bindings, the lack of water puddled round them* – and any noise is mentioned in terms of musical references – *man shouts violence in stark bass tones*. These are decisions which help give the character depth and create a sense of unity in the text.

Bringing it all together, writing it line by line on the page, was executed not by writing *about* the character, but by me *becoming* the character and acting out the unfolding story from that envisaged opening scene. In that first paragraph I wanted to explain what he was doing, intimate a back-story and a sense of melancholic desperation, and most of all his problem – *begin to yearn for the sharp taste of a beer* – hidden away in the phrases of a sentence so as to be hardly noticed by the reader.

The second paragraph I wanted to pertain to the sensuality music embraces, what I'd seen in my husband's colleague as his lips closed on the mouthpiece and he leaned into his saxophone with his eyes shut. Except that my character was not on a spot-lit stage, he was busking in an open shopping arcade with money at his feet, money that could be stolen from him in an instant. The last thing he would do would be to play a tune with his eyes closed, and as I wrote that second paragraph I knew I had the title.

Names are always problematic. Unlike the ones we carry, given to us by doting parents or taken on in marriage, the names of fictional characters have to offer an extra edge. As I began writing the story I had no idea what name my main character was travelling under, but I have enough experience to know that when a story is flowing I should trust it. Even so, when my lead character says to his younger self, *You don't know my name*, he was actually saying it to me. It was then, without a single beat pause, that his younger self replied *Marl*

Kerran and the scene finished. I gazed at my computer's screen, sliding the given name over my tongue. *Marl Kerran*. It sounded as much a stage name as a real name. The lazy *Marl*, the sharper *Kerran*. I accepted it. Sometimes writers just do.

Mickey Lyons was not so easy, either in himself or his name. I wanted him to be bold enough to speak to his idol, yet understanding enough to accept the man's current lifestyle and still hold him in awe. He needed to speak in a different manner to Marl Kerran, noticeably different, as many of their short exchanges would be without dialogue tags, a positive decision by me to set against the amount of detailed narrative coming via Kerran's thought processes. Although the dialogue of Mickey Lyons stayed more or less the same, the way it was presented, both the contractions and the syntax, was redrafted several times. If Kerran was thinking in the Queen's English, I didn't want Lyons to speak it.

The hell-hole of Marl Kerran's digs, thankfully I have no knowledge of first-hand. I wanted to make his present life intolerable, and to me lack of heat, lack of comfort, lack of food and the worst, constant noise, was as near a living hell as I could imagine for him at that time. It also served as a dark mirror to reflect back at him all he had once held – and what was being held out to him again, at a price. I wanted the reader to glean the back-story information, hold it up against the current information, and do what was being asked of Marl Kerran: make a choice.

When the story was completed I was pleased with it, but something didn't lie right. I read it, and fiddled, and read it again and again and again. It was some weeks later that I realised its problem. I'd written it as I write most of my fiction, using past tense. I'd asked copious questions of the characters and the setting, but taken for granted that the story should be written in past tense. Take nothing for granted. Moving the story into present tense gives the tone a clarity that Marl Kerran would demand from his music.

Over To You

Look at a piece of your own short fiction:

- Does the language used mirror the viewpoint character's occupation or mindset?
- Does the viewpoint character have a back-story?
- What would happen to the story if the tense was changed?

Try the exercise the way the Adult Education group did. List occupations of people you might see on the street. Pick one (preferably blindfold, with a pin) and build the character from scratch. Be that character. Who comes up to you, and why? Write that story.

An Introduction To

Contribution to Mankind

Contribution to Mankind was written due to a cold-hearted calculation. I wanted a story with my by-line in a particular paperback-sized anthology of short fiction. However, the anthology was only published quarterly, had a world-wide readership, and competition for acceptances was, to say the least, tight. Several of my stories had been returned with encouraging comments, from which I gleaned that my writing was up to scratch. The problem lay in their content. They simply weren't different enough to rise above other submissions.

My cold-hearted calculation? A filtering market study.

The anthology regularly listed all the genres it would accept. Horror was one. I delved through the copies stacked by my bed. In the three previous years not one Horror story had been printed.

Had I ever written Horror? No. Did I read Horror? I'd read a few novels – Stephen King, Richard Laymon – enough to know that I preferred the thinking-reader's horror to slasher gorefests, but I'd never read any short fiction in the genre.

I knew that MR James and Edgar Allan Poe were held in high regard and pulled books of their collected works from the library. It didn't take me long to realise that both might be vaunted masters of their artform, but they had written for a different readership in a different era. I had a look at an anthology of modern horror fiction. It was all a bit cutting-edge, all a bit weird for my taste and, I thought, for readers of my intended market.

I left the notion on the back-burner to concentrate on other writing.

Two things happened. I read a poem examining the term 'dead', and I was called to donate blood.

It was while I was waiting for my pint of life's liquor to filter into its plastic bag that I took particular interest in those round me doing the same. They were all ages, from all walks of life, there to do their bit to help their fellow man. No reason requested, none given.

This is inspiration. It's not a bolt out of the blue, but the slow embrace of separate facets and the writer's mind that recognises their potential.

Contribution to Mankind

Spaz passed the wrap across and I gave him the money.

'Sure you only want one?'

'No,' I said, 'I want six. Hell, let's not quibble about numbers. I'll have ten.'

I hadn't even given him The Look, and already his elbows were leaving the small bar table as he backed into his chair.

'Okay, okay,' he said. 'I can't guess your finances.'

I picked up my glass and dribbled the contents into my mouth. There wasn't even enough to coat my tongue.

'If you're looking for a source... Well, I might know of an off-licence, y'know, with an unguarded window.'

'And what use would that be to me?' I snapped. 'Think I'm an alckie?'

The little prat moved closer, sure of himself now.

'That's the beaut, isn't it? Could be there's an anxious buyer.'

I slid my empty glass across the table. He looked disconcerted and it made me smile. 'Buy me another and we'll talk about it.'

He didn't even try to argue, but dragged back his chair and limped towards the bar. I eyed his roll and sneered. He believed he had a charmed life, did Spaz, believed the sharks ignored the little fish. Silly bastard. Twice in plaster and still he thought he could fish the waters.

'Here he is! A round of applause for our hero!'

I looked to the clamour near the door. It was Tony mouthing off as usual, this time to a group from the old days. Tony was another one who'd never recognise his own name being called. And then I saw who *our hero* was and felt the tendons stand rigid in my neck. This wasn't his local any more; I'd driven the bastard out.

'Very funny,' Willans was saying. 'If you want to show some

appreciation of our contribution to mankind, get us in a beer.'

'Shouldn't it be weak tea?'

'Been there, done that, let the nurse hold my hand.'

Lascivious laughter rolled round the group and I knew there was no letting it pass.

'Listen to the pillock,' I called across. '*Contribution to mankind?* Be organising a fucking aid run to the Balkans next.'

That killed it. Willans peered over shoulders to see who had spoken and I gave him The Look in return. He soon shifted his gaze.

'It's your ten up, isn't it, Mike? Deserves one on the house, that.'

I turned my beadies on Don behind the bar, but he was already looking my way with a very flat expression. I marked it for future reference.

'Ten's nothing,' Willans said. 'It's the first that counts, and Jerry here has just passed the needle test.'

It was like listening to dogs puke. Jerry Davidson had all the hallmarks of a good wheelman: seconds into a Gti, and nerves the Iceman would prize when a blue light was tailgating him. He'd only been caught once, too, and now Willans had sunk his claws in. How many more of the bleating sheep would follow? All of them, probably, just as they had into that poxy soccer team he'd started. All the makings of a regular crusade, it had, with Jesus Bloody Christ at its head, shining example to the world.

When Spaz put a full glass in front of me I ignored him and took it to lean on the bar. Don gave me the warning eye, but I ignored him as well.

'Well, Jerry, congratulations. You've taken the first step to ensure your place in heaven. Has he got you to sign the red pledge, too, eh? Are you going to have some money-grubbing surgeon ripping out your heart before it's stopped beating? An eye here. A liver there. Sausage, mash and kidneys.'

'Leave it out, Sinclair.'

I turned my gaze on Willans, careful with The Look. I didn't want to spook him too soon.

'So, you've given ten, have you?' I said. 'Thought a body only carried eight. Shouldn't you be dead? Like Rob.'

'Give it up, Sinclair. That's six years behind us. I'm not rising to the bait any more.'

'Not rising?' I said. 'But you rose that night, didn't you, rose from the fucking dead. What was it? Twenty-five pints they pumped into you? Sounds about right. Still paying off the mortgage, I see.'

The others were behind him, not at his shoulder; leaderless, as ever. I bared my teeth and sneered to see what he'd do. He just stood there, the gutless wimp.

'Enough of that,' called Don.

I never even glanced Don's way. Don was all bluster. What was he going to do, call the Filth? The amount of gear they'd find carried in that place, they'd shut him down.

'It should have been Rob they dragged from the wreck, not you,' I said. 'Rob they pumped all those gallons of blood into, *not* you. You were supposed to be the fucking driver, not Rob. You were supposed to be looking out for him.'

I hadn't realised how quiet it had become until Don slammed the baseball bat down onto the bar.

'I said *enough*. If you put as much effort into raising money for charity as you do into your hate, your brother would have some sort of decent memorial. But no, you'd rather the likes of Jerry here follow him into an early grave. And doing what? *Joy*-riding. I don't see how it's brought much joy round here.'

Don didn't even recognise The Look when I shot it across, he was in such a flood. He'd remember it when it topped out, though, I'd see to that.

But what was the point? The exchange was going nowhere. Willans wasn't going to bite, not like in the old days when he'd sooner knock your teeth down your throat than look at you. Getting old, that was the problem, getting old and got his own personal brand of religion.

I prodded a finger just the once in his chest. Every rib seemed to show through his T-shirt. The flab had deserted him, just like his balls.

'You should take more care of yourself, Mikey. All this running's wearing you out. What is it this time? Equipment for the Infirmary? Research into crippling diseases? Here...' I tossed a coin across at him. It bounced off his bony chest and fell to the floor between us. 'Put me down for a slice. We can't have Don, here, thinking I don't support lost causes.'

I downed the rest of the pint in one and smacked the glass on the bar. I'd hoped Willans might give me reason to smash it into his face, but there was always tomorrow. I'd waited six years. I wasn't in any hurry.

About a week later Spaz came across with the info on the off-licence deal. I did some quiet digging and it seemed clean enough. I wasn't too worried about Spaz, anyway. Despite his lack between the ears he knew full well that his time in plaster would be nothing compared to what would happen if he crossed me.

The place was a small set-up in one of the closer villages. Working out of the city had its compensations. The Filth took longer to arrive, for one, and iron window grilles and concrete bollards set beyond the shop's front were almost unheard of.

I'd picked up a van - not to do the job, that was set for the following night - just to drive the route we were going to use. These things always look fine on paper, but it's amazing how many times you can come across roadworks on these narrow lanes, or a pile of straw bales sticking out from the verge.

Dusk was falling, not enough to hit the lights, but close enough so that I'd be travelling back with them on, as I'd intended. Anyway, I saw him, Willans, loping along what passed for the gutter in a skinny pair of tracksuit bottoms and a reflective yellow vest. I didn't realise it was him until I was passing, and even then I was a good half mile ahead before it registered.

Willans. Running on his ownsome in the middle of bloody nowhere. Willans. Running on the road in the dusk.

I turned the van and headed back.

I came upon him almost at once, and slowed the engine to a crawl, hanging back to watch his rhythmic action. Left foot, right foot. Left foot, right foot. Left foot, right foot. Almost like a heartbeat. My heartbeat as it rose in anticipation.

Why didn't he hear the engine? Then I realised: there was something attached to a belt round his waist. An iPod. I smiled. I couldn't help it.

'For you, Rob.' And I gunned the engine.

He heard me at the last moment. I saw the beginning of a turn of his head, but the edge of the bumper caught him, or the wing, and he disappeared from my view.

I pulled up gently and looked through the mirrors. He was prone, for certain, but in the failing light I couldn't see more. And I wanted to see more. I wanted to see what I'd seen on the slab in the morgue when I'd identified Rob.

I reversed the van and opened the driver's door.

He was laid partly on the verge in the shadow of the hedge, his arms angled as if he were still running. The iPod was kicking out its tune as if nothing had happened. I could hear it as I approached. It threw me for a moment, made me think that I hadn't hit him after all.

There didn't seem to be any blood. I didn't believe that and got down on my haunches to peer closer.

There wasn't any blood, not even a graze that I could see. That wasn't right, wasn't fair on Rob.

The music was getting on my nerves. There should have been blood and there wasn't and the damned noise from that thing was driving me crazy. I put out a hand to switch it off and saw that there was a polythene cover over it. Inside the polythene cover was a tenner and a credit card. Willans was running round the countryside with a note and a credit card strapped to his iPod. Had he been expecting some farmer to draw up and offer him a neat deal on hamburger?

I realised my mistake as soon as I pulled them free. The card was the bastard's red pledge, his organ donor card. Rob didn't get any organs. Rob didn't even get any blood.

I was holding it, staring at it, when I heard the faint wisps of a groan. The bastard wasn't dead. Then his eyes flickered open and he looked at me. I looked straight back at him.

'Ssssin...clair..?'

'Yeah, it's Sinclair. How you feeling, Willans?'

He blinked, and gave a faint stab at a frown. I'd dislodged something, that was certain.

'Can you get up?'

There was a second or two while his mouth tried to work.

'No.'

'You just lie there and listen to your music.' I replaced the earphones and his limbs seemed to twitch at the sudden injection of sound. 'Won't be long,' I said, but I don't think he heard me.

Once in the driving seat I fired the engine, slipped it into gear, and reversed over him. Like hitting a kerb, it was, with the nearside rear. The front jumped, too. For good measure I slid into first and pulled forward slowly. There wasn't as much resistance the second time. Willans could donate all he owned, but who'd want a bucket of sludge?

The red pledge was still in my fingers as I pulled away. I smiled at it and slipped it into my jacket with the tenner. It would make an interesting souvenir, a decent lever, too, I shouldn't wonder, shown to someone who knew him and was getting out of line.

I didn't use that van for the job the following night. I picked up a neat red Transit. Handled a treat through the plate glass. The buyer was waiting at the rendezvous point, and without hardly a word being spoken, the cases were exchanged for cash at the agreed rate. I was still nursing my share when news of Willans' demise caught up with me. In the pub everyone was crying into their beer. It was pathetic.

'They wouldn't let me identify him,' Jerry kept saying. 'Said I was too young.'

'So who did identify him?' I asked.

'Don. And then it was only his shirt. And his iPod. Flatter than a pancake, Don said his iPod was. And covered in blood.'

I glanced across at the bar. Don was looking directly at me.

'Hit 'n' run?' I asked.

'Bleeding joy-rider. Out of his head, too, from what the police said.' He lifted a finger and pointed at me. 'And I don't want even the suspicion of a sneer from you or you're out on your ear and you're never coming back in.'

I kept The Look under wraps, but he wouldn't have noticed if I'd given it full vent. Already his gaze was searing round the bar.

'As for the rest of you miserable bastards, you can all take due warning. There's going to be no more dealing under this roof. And if I hear of any of you taking cars I'll personally see to it that the Filth hits you hard. Mike changed his colours and you can too.' He turned and slapped his hand against the sponsorship totals Willans had pinned beside the optics.

'This isn't going to finish just because Mike's gone. The soccer team is going to carry on, and the Orthopaedic ward is going to get its equipment cheque.'

He dipped under the counter and brought up a tall glass jar. 'You can all do your bit right now and put a note in there for Mike.'

The jar got pushed towards Spaz and the prat hobbled round the silent tables taking donations. I slipped in the tenner I'd taken from Willans. Even he would have appreciated the irony in that.

*

Life got back to some sort of normality over the next few weeks. The team lost three matches in a row and I heard that only half the players turned up for the fourth so it was called off. Spaz started dealing under the table again, and Don only moaned a little when he heard one of the boys boasting about a Ford he'd boosted. Jerry moped about a bit, but I took him under my wing, so to speak, and he started coming round just as Spaz collared me for another out of town off-licence deal. Our buyer, evidently, was running out of supplies.

The Nissan was a snip to get into, and despite its age handled well. The target was a small one-manned supermarket in some god-forsaken place I hadn't known existed. No grille on the window; no concrete bollards out front. Just sitting there asking for it. I even parked up and went in for a pack of twenty. The guy was still sorting his delivery. Cases of whisky and vodka were piled in the storeroom doorway. There wasn't a soul. I could have done him then, on my own, if I'd wanted. Proved one thing, though. Spaz's information was top notch.

On the way back I gave the Nissan some throttle. It purred like a pussy cat round the bends, though the lights were shuttered a little low for my liking.

Keeping an eye on the route on the way out, I'd not taken much interest in the interior. Now I switched on the radio and pushed in the CD that was sitting in the deck. I recognised the song, some tune I'd heard countless times before, but as it played it niggled at the back of my mind, as if I should have been able to place it spot on. And then I did. It had been playing on Willans' iPod when I'd trashed him.

'Ha! Willans! You'll have to try harder than that to haunt me, y'bastard.'

I reached out, glancing down to hit Eject. My finger connected, the music cut, and I looked up through the windscreen to see Willans caught in the dipped heads like a rabbit, except that he was running towards me, not away, and I could still hear that tune, distant and tinny, as if it was coming from his iPod.

And he just kept on running towards the car, those skinny legs pounding, that reflective yellow vest bouncing up and down as the headlights shone full in his unblinking eyes, full in his toothy, grinning face. Automatically I moved my foot to brake, but hell... I'd already killed the bastard. My foot hit the gas again and the windscreen shattered into a million spinning fragments.

'*Ssssin...clair...*'

'Blood pressure's dropping.'

'*Sinclair...*'

'Don't lose him. We mustn't lose him.'

'*Come on, Sinclair. Don't fart about. I know you can hear me.*'

'*W- Willans?*'

'*Ah, the man himself. How y'doing, Sinclair?*'

'He's going, I tell you. If you're doing it, do it fast.'

'He's lasted this long. We can't let him slip away now. Where the hell's that equipment?'

'*What's- What's going on?*'

'*Take a look. You've still got an eye.*'

It was an odd sensation. There was a pinpoint of light that grew until it filled my vision with a blur of white, and then everything drew into focus.

'That's it. He's left us.'

I was looking down on heads, and arms, and the bright reflections from stainless steel, and in the midst of it all, in the middle of the dancing arms and silver tubes...

'*Argh!*'

I was lying naked on an operating table, hardly a blemish below my shoulders, my head looking as if the right half had been hacked away with a spade.

'*Sorry about the eye, Sinclair. Truly, I am.*'

The smell was unbelievable. I wanted to retch.

'You're okay now. Don't worry about it.'

'What- What happened?'

'You know what happened.'

I started to shake my head, but the weight was all wrong, and I thought it was going to fall off.

'Where have you been? Get that set up. We've not much time.'

'You- You were running into me.'

'Me? Now how could I do that, Sinclair? I'm dead.'

'Clear on my call.'

'The yellow vest.'

'A JCB parked on the verge. You swung round the bend too wide and the bucket took your head off. Or nearly off. Sorry about the eye, though. A waste that.'

'Clear!'

Pain hit me in the chest and shot down my limbs to fry my fingers and toes. I fought for my breath, for my stomach contents, for my sanity, and then a fire gripped my throat and worked its way down inside my chest. I tried to speak, to scream, but couldn't make a sound.

'No need to panic, Sinclair. Just watch them work. You'll stabilize in a minute or two. Great what medical science can do these days, don't you think?'

Below me, the heads and arms eased away from the table and I saw that a thick tube had been inserted directly into my throat.

'What about next of kin?'

'No one's come forward. That bit wasn't filled in.'

'Oh, look... You're getting a blood transfusion, too. We're the same group, y'know. Ironic, isn't it? You're probably getting a pint of mine.'

The stench grew thicker, more cloying.

'You know why you're getting a transfusion, don't you?'

There was a tinny sound I'd thought was part of the equipment below, but it was resolving into a muffled tune.

'To keep your organs alive.'

I turned then, turned through my blind side to look at Willans at my shoulder. I screamed, or tried to. He was grinning with a lopsided half mouth, two untouched teeth in his upper gum sunk into a plastic earphone still pumping music. The rest of his head was a pulped mass, bloody gore fanning from fissures in his skull, congealed globules suspended from an eye socket. Where his nose had been was the imprint of a tyre tread.

'Hello, Sinclair. Nice to see you again, with my one good eye.'

The white orb stared at me from his cheek, held there by a curdle of blood and its own retaining stalk.

An elongated arm lifted from a shattered shoulder, manoeuvring with the dexterity of a wayward tentacle, flattened here, there protruding splintered bone. It lifted to grasp me in a grotesque semblance of friendship. Willans' other arm looped metres of glistening intestines close to his burst abdomen and shattered ribs. The smell was more than I could bear.

And then the pain began again and Willans pointed down below. They were taking out my kidneys and I could feel each cut of the knife.

My belly collapsed upon itself as my liver and pancreas followed. I felt each crack of my ribs as they tore into my chest, their hands lifting out my lungs in turn and severing my heart.

'One last request, is there? Something you want to see?'

I watched as they gathered round my head. Saw the scalpel rise. Saw no more.

'Oops, too late.'

The blackness was total, and out of the blackness came the stench of Willans and the tinny sound of the iPod's tune. I felt his smashed arm wrap itself round my hollow chest, his splintered bones interlocking with my loose-hinged ribs.

'Now the fun starts, Sinclair. At least eight lives to be renewed. Could be ten. Sorry I won't be round to see it, but I'm *being called into the light.'*

A clammy hand patted my shoulder.

'Not to worry, though. You won't be in limbo for long. Once you're hooked into your recipients you'll feel their every little wheeze, their every little ache until, one by one, you feel their death throes.

'But look on the bright side. They may be donors themselves. With the leaps being made in medical science you could go on for decades, for centuries, before it's your turn to step into the light.'

The tinny music grew loud in my ear, the fetid stench heavy in my nostrils.

'Good job you picked up my red pledge, eh, Sinclair? Think of the contribution that would have been lost to mankind.'

Commentary

As with *Shared With The Light* that precedes it, *Contribution to Mankind* relies heavily on Tone to portray the main character, but in this instance vulnerability is not being conveyed. My thinking was to portray Sinclair's character traits via his own self image – and we all think we're okay, right?

First person viewpoint was a necessity to gain such a narrow, biased view, and I made a decision on the level of chattiness of his delivery so that his affability would be at odds with both the words he uttered and his inner commentary. I was aiming to make the reader wary while still being drawn in to Sinclair's world, to view it through his eyes and by his moral compass. I didn't want him to be a sociopath, or even a psychopath. That would make him a monster, easily labelled and dismissed as such by readers as being different from themselves. I wanted him to be someone readers might meet on the street, or in the supermarket. The horrors people are capable of inflicting upon others knows no bounds, and very few of these people are true monsters. They're half a step left of me and you.

To understand such a person's thinking, to make him able to justify his actions as normal, or his victims as "asking for it", a writer needs to follow the line of the person's back-story to see what made him the way he is, and what conscious decisions to define himself he made along the way. To me, this equates to Nature versus Nurture.

The opening setting, the main setting, is a public house. To Sinclair it is his local so it doesn't warrant a description, but can you, the reader, describe its interior? Where is it situated? Is it, for instance, situated in a leafy suburb?

This is describing by omission, description by glancing reflections off the character base, which in turn reflect on the characters. No one in this pub is wearing an Armani suit or sipping a cocktail. There again, no one is speaking the way they should in the real world.

Another decision was to have all parties talking the Queen's English. There might be the usual word contractions, but not the broken phrasing or slang anticipated of this group. Sinclair is the only person who swears, another anomaly, which I use to bolster the contempt he feels for everyone, but does he use the words, or use them with the regularity, he would in real life?

This decision was made partly because of the market's constraints, and partly because profanities written in the profusion that would be uttered by these people would render the story unreadable and the narrative text out of kilter. One aspect alone cannot be made to seem realistic; it has to be applied across the fiction equally - and that is no mean feat. Few writers pen true realism. The trick is for the writer to make the reader believe in the world depicted, not render it as reality. Like truth, there is no such definable entity, only personal experience.

Sinclair's nature was to rise above his peers in some way, but not to lift himself from his environment. Yet he detests his environment, detests his peers, proving to himself that he's better by scoring illusory points and taking enjoyment from baiting those round him. This is self-nurturing, a form of aggrandisement. If I'd been writing a novel, even a novella, I would have delved into his psyche and background in far more detail, but for the length of a short story this level of detail was enough for me to know he could run on his own.

A catalyst was needed for the story. This is why building a plausible environment is so important. It produces catalysts that are embedded in the fabric of the fiction, not introduced as an extraneous entity that needs to be bolted in and smoothed to fit. The type of environment, the type of people depicted, spawn joy-riding. Joy-riders over-reach themselves, they have accidents, they rarely joy-ride alone.

Willans was chosen by me to be Sinclair's soul-mate separated by a near-death experience and a conscious decision to redefine his life. Through Sinclair, I allude to what Willans had once been like. ...*Willans wasn't going to bite, not like in the old days when he'd sooner knock your teeth down your throat than look at you.* With Sinclair's nature already established, and the pub environment growing, there are enough pointers for readers to fill in the blanks. It wasn't necessary to lead them through a character study. Doing so would have killed the fiction by making it turgid.

The only other person to mention is Don, the manager or owner of the pub. Although I envisioned him as quite a bit older than his regulars there's no reason why this should be mentioned. He is one of them while being apart from them. He turns a blind eye to the drug dealing and the stealing of cars. He'd like to keep the peace in his pub but in truth can't summon the energy to lay down rules and enforce them. I use him to convey bits of back-story and off-page action that readers need to be aware of but that would seem odd coming from Sinclair.

Not all short fiction needs to be set up like this – more often back-story and character delineation are knitted in during the unfolding of the forward storyline – but due to the matey tone I'd chosen for Sinclair's narrative I needed the forward storyline to be as clear of explanations as possible.

It is this clarity, this ordinariness in his delivery of what transpires on the country lane, which conveys the horror of what he does. Did I deliberately mute it by foreshadowing retribution when he pocketed Willan's organ donor card along with his money? Not deliberately, but it would need a particularly unobservant reader not to connect the two. Did I think it would help readers stay with the story, knowing that Sinclair was liable to get his "just desserts"? Not necessarily.

For the story I needed the donor card to be mentioned, but foreshadowing of any type needs to be deftly applied and this acts as a waved flag. I do foreshadow – did you notice? – when Sinclair mentions the possibility of ...*roadworks on these narrow lanes, or a pile of straw bales sticking out from the verge*...and again when he mentions that the headlights of the car he steals are ...*shuttered a little low for my liking*... Therefore when the windscreen shatters as he drives into the digger, although it should come as much as a surprise to readers as it does to Sinclair, it fits.

I have no familiarity with out-of-body experiences, but a little research gave the scenario in the operating theatre. With their roles reversed, I wanted Willans to convey a gleeful enthusiasm for what was occurring below, tempered by a muted sense of triumph at justice being seen to be done.

The depth of description of Willans was deliberate, but coupled with his bright chat, does it remain within the bounds of horror, or has it strayed into black comedy? I guess that depends on the individual reader.

These two stories, *Shared With The Light* and *Contribution to Mankind* demonstrate the importance and versatility of Tone. Don't ignore this valuable writer's tool. And yes, the story was published in that quarterly anthology.

Over to You

Don't worry, I'm not suggesting you write Horror; I'm suggesting you follow the path I used to bring together two or three unrelated aspects, and fuse them into a story idea.

Choose a genre; it helps to focus the mind. From a book of poetry, pick a page at random and study the given poem. What is the poem about? List words or phrases which come to mind.

At a given time, focus on your surroundings and then focus on the people sharing those surroundings with you. Who are they? Why are they there? You don't need to visit a special place to do this. Set an alarm on your mobile phone, or some other self-indicator, and when it sounds take five minutes to observe and interrogate whatever surroundings you find yourself in, and the people there with you. Finding yourself alone is still an acceptable answer. Commit all you can to memory or, if you have time, make notes.

During a spare few minutes write your memories as listed phrases, or read through your notes and add to them. Read through the list several times during the next day or so. Re-read the poem, and the notes made from it. The repetitive nature of this allows the subconscious to do its work.

During your next period of writing highlight words or phrases to which you are drawn – for whatever reason. Blend these into a character, male or female, young or old. Give this person a single word emotion, for instance: happy, sad, angry, disappointed...

Follow the line of this character's back-story until you come upon a reason, or set of reasons, for why the character is feeling this emotion in this place. What is the character going to do about this? In that question is your story.

Don't be discouraged if you find this difficult. If your brain isn't used to making connections, it'll fight every step. Practising does help to grease the wheels.

As well as leading to a piece of fiction, you are attuning your own emotional antennae to that of a writer's.

What Constitutes Women's Fiction?

Women's Fiction is a huge and somewhat arbitrary genre label arcing across fiction that is perceived as of interest to more female readers than male readers. Human relationships, not romance, is its core component, therefore siblings, parents, and colleagues from the work or home environment, play central roles. The main character has no need to be female, yet often is due to pressure from publishers. There is no necessity for a universal "happy ever after" ending but, in line with most genres, there needs to be a conclusion that satisfies readers' expectations.

Short fiction written within the Women's Fiction genre can cover themes equally suited to genres ranging from literary to crime to romance to SF and fantasy, depending on the slant and tone used. As ever, these are dictated largely by the intended market. A regional magazine will rarely vie for the same type of story that a magazine aimed at young mothers might publish, and the same applies to digital markets. The key is not always in the stories printed, but in the advertisements and non-fiction articles contained within, making up part of the writer's market study.

With the general contraction in the print magazine field, and its focus on celebrity lifestyles and features requiring shorter attention spans, writing competitions for short fiction have come more to the fore. Don't concentrate solely within your own national boundary. The English-speaking, English-reading, on-line world is integrating fast, and users are adjusting to communication across different time zones. With the continuing rise in ownership of e-readers and tablet computers, downloadable magazine-style journals are flourishing, and anthologies are once again seeing ascendancy, if not necessarily in print form.

The following four stories, all Women's Fiction written for the print magazine market, have been chosen for their subtle differences rather than to illustrate the wide variety of the genre.

An Introduction To

Permanently Portugal

Writers tend to fall into two main camps: those who Tell a story and those who Show a story to the reader. I am, by nature, a Show writer. I like to choose a viewpoint character, get under that character's skin and feel his every wheezing breath, her every fluttering heartbeat. But not every story lends itself to this approach. Sometimes a story needs to be Told because if it was Shown it would show too much at once.

The choice of Viewpoint should never be made lightly: first person, third person singular, third person multiple, second person, true omniscient, selected omniscient… each carries with it a mechanism for distancing the reader from the action, a mechanism that can be reeled out or in as the writer dictates.

To decide on a Structure is to decide how best to convey the tale. Few stories open at the very beginning and carry on until the very end. Most start somewhere in the first third, bringing the reader up to speed by a subtle use of back-story before pausing at the axis point and pressing for the finish. Some start at the end and have events leading to that point unfold in a series of flashbacks.

Permanently Portugal was written specifically to fulfil my wish to write a calendar story. The calendar I chose is not dated, but covers a week marked by named days to create a tension in the unfolding of events, a deadline to be met or beaten.

What do we do that covers a week but is marked by named days? We take a holiday.

Permanently Portugal

They landed in Portugal on the Wednesday. Michael had been edgy on the plane, as he always was, and when James was late collecting them from the airport Miriam had difficulty keeping the peace. Once father and son were united, though, the atmosphere changed, and by the time they reached James' apartment the stress was evaporating.

That evening, and all the following day, the three of them revisited old haunts and met old acquaintances, Miriam consciously slipping further into the background as the two men bonded once more. By Friday her time was her own.

Her first stop was at the Tourist Information office, her second a sunny table at a street café in the main square to read the gathered literature. There she was drawn into conversation with a couple from Bristol.

'You're not here on your own?' asked the woman, shocked.

'Oh, no,' said Miriam. 'At home I care for my husband. Our son lives here and he shoulders the responsibility when we come so that I get a break.'

Miriam never went into details and deftly changed the subject, discovering that her acquaintances were attending an evening of traditional entertainment. She'd been to one before, but accepted their invitation to join them. Miriam had a thoroughly enjoyable time, full of music and laughter, and she felt the old anxieties begin to fall away.

The apartment was quiet when she returned, and she tip-toed to bed. She tip-toed out the following morning to the accompaniment of James' and Michael's gentle snoring, and spent the early part of the day on the beach before the sun grew too hot.

In the afternoon she took a coach trip through mountain villages laced with bougainvillaea, marvelling at the russet colours glowing in the landscape, and at fruiting lemon trees over-hanging white-washed walls. It was so peaceful, so unlike home. There were rooms for rent and villas for hire, but she didn't make enquiries. A mountain village might be picturesque, but as a relocation site it was hardly practical.

On Sunday the church bells rang for the Lord's Day and the Saint's feast, and Miriam followed the parade up and down the narrow streets of the old town, as bands played and the local people waved streamers. The celebrations were better than even the guidebook had suggested, and Miriam was so pleased she'd been able to book their flights to coincide with it.

Sitting on a bench in a tiny, fountained, square, she sampled portions of home-baked breads and succulent cheeses the householders offered as a blessing upon themselves and upon the recipients. In another square she accepted delicate pastries filled with nuts and dripping honey. Each small quadrangle held a new delight, and she was carried on the tide of people to fire-crackers and juggling clowns, to a cup of local wine and a bright lapel sticker, to a colourful mime where the audience oohed and aahed – from one to the next until fireworks shattered the night's dark sky. With aching feet and a happy heart, she headed back to the tourist area and James' apartment.

In a shop window along the way, a notice written in English caught her eye. She read it as she passed, and then returned to read it slowly *...includes one bedroom accommodation with terrace.* She read the details several times, trying to find fault, finally wending her way to her own bed in a more thoughtful mood.

By Monday, unable to survive the stark realities of daylight, the notion of moving permanently to Portugal had returned to its soft romantic fantasy. Miriam toured the cathedral in the morning, falling into a discussion with two French women over the 14th century murals. It was the first time she'd been able to put knowledge gained at her evening class to use, and she was proud that she could hold her own in the conversation.

Ignoring gaudy cafés and noisy bars on the harbour front, she took salad and charcoal-grilled sardines for lunch, delighted that her faltering Portuguese was understood. She didn't dally, though, at the sun-kissed table. She felt the need to keep occupied, and toured the air-conditioned museum that didn't close for the siesta.

In the late afternoon she bought the local English language newspaper and scanned the classifieds. As she'd hoped, there was the notice that had appeared in the shop window. A sense of excitement returned. She could do this, she told herself, if she had the courage.

She had to be sensible though, she knew that. Living in a foreign country was not the same as taking an extended holiday. If she miscalculated the finances there would be no Social Security payments to fall back on. Was it worth the risk? Could Michael cope with the upheaval? Could she embrace another way of life?

By Tuesday morning she was decided. With one day left before she and Michael flew back, where was the harm in making enquiries?

She felt nervous telephoning, as if attempting her first interview, but the gentleman spoke excellent English so her carefully copied phrases weren't needed.

When she met him he was courtesy itself, introducing her to his wife and children, and to his aging mother. The apartment he showed her was small, but comfortable, the adorning paintings from the hand of an accomplished artist. Double doors opened onto a wide terrace shaded by an orange tree, and gave, to Miriam's delight, a vista of red pantile roofs climbing slowly up the hillside.

'Do you paint?' she was asked.

Miriam laughed. 'Only to emulsion the dining room wall.' But she'd always wanted to try, and here she felt she might.

They spoke of life in England, and of life in Portugal, but all the time Miriam's heart was aflutter. Was she brave enough to grasp the change?

'I'll think about it,' she said.

For a sleepless night Miriam thought about it. Early Wednesday morning she took a walk in the municipal gardens to breathe the fragrances and clear the clamour from her head. She and Michael were flying at one-thirty. A decision was needed now. She made the call and returned to James' apartment, resigned.

'You stupid cow!' Michael exploded. 'Where've you been 'til this hour? The cases have to be packed yet.'

'She's done it on purpose,' snapped James, 'so she won't have time to clean the flat.'

Miriam said nothing. As she'd done all week, she tip-toed between discarded food cartons and empty beer cans, this time to start her chores.

Trapped between the aeroplane window and her grumbling husband, Miriam gazed down at the disappearing countryside. If she could work shifts in a care home, she could assist one disabled English painter living with her son and Portuguese daughter-in-law. And the lady, Chloe, had been so easy to talk to, so joyous in her own life.

As Michael demanded his first lager from the stewardess, Miriam sat back in her seat and put on the headphones. A fortnight to bed Michael back into his pub and bookies routine, give in her notice and draw her secreted savings, and she would be sitting on a sunlit terrace with a book on her lap, perhaps even with an easel at her side.

She closed her eyes to breathe deeply and, for her, the air was scented with orange blossom.

Commentary

This is a Told story, to the extent that there pervades the impression that an invisible narrator is filtering, and condensing, events. It also plays into the hands of readers who jump to conclusions on the flimsiest of evidence.

I, as the writer, never lie in conveying the tale. Miriam, as the main character, never lies in either her recorded dialogue or her summarized discussions, or in the description of what she actually does. I, and therefore she, simply do not give the whole picture, and we can do this because of the distance readers are kept from the action via the use of selected omniscient viewpoint.

I position the boundaries early, as a writer always should, so that readers automatically acclimatise to the restrictions of the world view being offered. The choice of *They* to open the first line is a deliberate attempt to set the distance that readers stand from the action. Consider how much chummier, and therefore closer, the story would have read if it had begun *Miriam and Michael landed in Portugal on Wednesday* rather than the bald *They landed in Portugal on the Wednesday*. Note, too, *the Wednesday*. By the judicious use of adding a definite article, I move the emphasis from the abstract *They* to the named day, and so start the calendar sequence.

You're not convinced? Nor should you be. A story is not a single piece of coloured glass held up against the light. It is many pieces of differently coloured glass of differing thickness, layered, both individually and in groups, in front of a roving light which dims and brightens. A story conveyed on a single piece of glass, coloured or not, is a story without depth or nuance. This should not be what you are aiming to produce.

As the story opens one piece of glass is put into place; the light shines at one intensity. As the story progresses pieces of coloured glass are added, the changing intensity of light altering the hues of the combined glass. It is the writer's job to control the adding of the glass and the intensity of the light, the readers' job to make sense of the building picture slowly coming into focus.

Many pieces of glass are added during those first couple of paragraphs, when readers are releasing their hold on their own reality and engaging with the reality of the fiction. It is not the main character who is mentioned first by name, but the two men, thus making her subordinate in the group hierarchy.

Take particular note of the names. These were not chosen on a whim, but were selected with care. All three are ancient. In particular, the two male names have a long tradition of stability and acceptance, and thus carry less emotional baggage for the reader than names more in keeping with current fashion. This is why they are given in full. Mike or Mickey, Jim or Jimmy hold connotations I didn't want readers to pursue. I wanted Michael and James to appear ordinary, almost bland. Usually I take exception when a student matches the names of characters, but I chose Miriam to purposely do just that, to be married to Michael and live in his shadow, M&M.

Characters must be undergoing problems, recognised by them or not, for a story to succeed. Early in the first paragraph I allude to problems that Miriam is coping with. *Michael had been edgy on the plane, as he always was,* is hardly a major problem; many people don't like flying. But an extra dimension is added with *and when James was late collecting them from the airport Miriam had difficulty keeping the peace.* I seed the thought that perhaps there is something wrong with Michael. During the second paragraph, and the second day, *the two men bonded once more* and Miriam slips into the background, again suggesting something slightly off-key, while re-emphasising her lesser role in the hierarchy.

By the third paragraph, the beginning of Miriam's perceived

freedom, I drip-feed the first indication of description, *a sunny table at a street café* – a positive, bright, image – following it immediately by a veiled explanation of why she is on her own. And why shouldn't her explanation be veiled? She is talking to complete strangers. Do you go into detail about your family life with complete strangers? Perhaps you do if you are happy with it, if you have nothing to hide. People in abusive relationships rarely do, and some go to inordinate lengths not only to project a facade, but to believe the façade they project to others.

Within that line of dialogue, though, readers pick up what is required to strengthen the belief that Michael is in some way either ill or disabled. Readers sympathise, and are hooked.

This is the first turning point in the story, the moment the drip-fed indication of description begins to change into a torrent of light and colour and texture as the doors open onto a rose-tinted world of what life might offer in a foreign country, and with it the fantasy of living somewhere different, of being someone different, that readers can embrace.

Subtle use of back-story shows that Miriam is already "someone different" as she falls into discussion about the cathedral's murals and takes pride in being able to articulate new-found knowledge. This is a double-whammy as far as characterisation is concerned. By showing what is new about her, it gives a glimpse of what is old. She is making an effort to be someone else through education, by learning the language, by eating with the locals instead of being associated with the tourists on the harbour front. She is straddling two worlds.

The awkwardness this brings is acknowledged by Miriam in a bout of inner turmoil. She worries about finances, about how Michael will cope with the upheaval. There is, note, no mention of expecting any help from James to ease the transition, and this very omission should sound alarm bells for readers, though it rarely does.

As the paragraphs pass, so do the days. Miriam needs to make a decision. She can't bring herself to do that, it is too momentous for her, so she placates her desire by *where was the harm in making enquiries?* Readers, though, are already ahead of the action, and when those enquiries lead to courteous people and an inspiring view, they will Miriam to grasp the opportunity, in effect to live happily ever after, thereby fulfilling their own hazy fantasies of leaving the rat-race and living a more leisurely life.

From a writer's stance, this is far too glib. Readers shouldn't be able to see ahead with such confidence. A spanner needs to be thrown into the works. So I throw a spanner: Miriam prevaricates. Even when faced down by the ticking clock, she can't make the decision. When she does communicate with the Portuguese household, readers aren't a party to it, in keeping with the viewpoint and distance chosen for the story, but see only Miriam's attitude: she's *resigned*. While readers are pondering this they are hit by the reality of Miriam's life in the form of the aggressive dialogue from her husband and son.

The scene break is most important. Throughout the story the changes in days and time have been effected by the use of summary, easing readers from one to another. Here, the break is deliberate and brutal. It affords readers the space to mentally reassess what has been read and pinpoint where and why they jumped to the wrong conclusions.

Hindsight is a wonderful gift. It enables us to read between the lines with perception. Was Michael just *edgy* on the plane? What *peace* had Miriam difficulty in keeping when there was a delay at the airport? Which *old haunts* and *old acquaintances* did the three of them revisit immediately upon arrival? How were father and son *bonding*? How do the answers match what Miriam told the couple from Bristol?

I make much of her tip-toeing into a quiet apartment late one evening, and *tip-toeing out the following morning* to the men's snores. The assumption I wanted readers to take is that the pair had been asleep the night before. Hindsight grants that this couldn't be further from the truth, hence my reiterating her action of *tip-toeing* across the room, this time widening the visual lens to include the littered floor, so as to pull the beginning of the story closer to the ending.

Having conjured this picture of the obnoxious males in her life and so given reason for her dreams of escape, of becoming someone else, Miriam is written not only sitting on a plane returning to the UK, but *trapped* between the window giving a view of her Utopia, and her grumbling, beer-guzzling, husband. She has not escaped, and is returning to the continuance of an unrewarding life.

And yet...

Readers have to make another minor adjustment as it is realised that a decision has been made, a decision right for Miriam, and that she is, after all, going to grasp her chance at a new life.

No matter how a story is written, questions need to be asked of the elements to ensure they hang together:

Why didn't Miriam dump Michael years before? Why did she marry him at all? Most of us are products of our own and others' expectations. If her upbringing had led her to expect this sort of treatment, then she would have accepted it. I don't describe any of the characters physically so that their ages are as fluid as each reader needs to settle them into an age group.

However, consider this: if Michael, and in his shadow, James, were so contemptuous of Miriam, wouldn't their language have been more abusive? In reality, certainly it would, but in the fiction the depth of that abuse would be determined by the market the story was aimed at, just as it was in *Contribution to Mankind*.

Why Portugal and not the more in-keeping Costas of Spain with their stereotypical loud-mouthed UK ex-pats? Because I felt that would be giving away too many clues to the reader.

Does the story stand up to be counted? I'm happy with it, happy with everything except that last scene on the plane.

Despite the story selling as read, that scene has been taken out, put back in, revised and rewritten, but it continues to niggle. I suspect it holds too much explanatory information – rather like the denouement meeting in the library characteristic of an Agatha Christie novel. Yet it is in keeping with the distanced, selected omniscient conveyance chosen for the story. There can be no elongated or highly emotional ending that would fit a straight third-person viewpoint. When boundaries are set at the outset, they need to be adhered to throughout, including the ending, so as to maintain a balance correct for that story.

Over To You

If your tendency is to always write a story with a straightforward construction, try using a calendar structure to push back the boundaries of your comfort zone. If you forever write within your known strengths, how do you improve your skills levels?

A calendar story doesn't have to use a series of named days; it can use hours, weeks or months. Choose a time-span and consider what sequence of events would be suited to it. For instance, an hours format could involve the logistics of readying for an event, either personal or public; a weeks format could involve a ship calling at ports enroute to its destination.

List all potential ideas, no matter how tentative, as often one idea sparks another. When your output has been exhausted, choose one. Ask questions of the idea. Think through possible answers using *who*, *when*, *what*, *where*, *how* and *why*. A ship could be a liner, a tanker, a schooner, a barge on a canal.

Next, list a series of *what if..?* possibilities to jolt the expected run of events: illness, accident, weather change, attack by vandals... Again, pick one and think through the consequences. Somewhere in the inner workings of your mind a character should be emerging, a character with problems. Give him or her some breathing space, and let that person live on the page.

Note: a calendar story looks forwards, making sense of events as they unfold; a diary or journal story looks backwards, making sense of events that have already happened. So now you have two structures to consider. Give them your best shot. You might be pleasantly surprised by the results.

An Introduction To

An Interesting Day In The Office

This story was written specifically to fulfil a request from a women's magazine for twist-in-the-tale fiction.

The problem when writing such a prescribed format, and especially when heralded beneath that banner as the magazine did, the reader is primed to be on the look-out for signals that in a normal story would be absorbed as a component of the whole. It is part of the reader's enjoyment to study these signals so as to work out the twist before the end of the story, and, as with word quizzes, once a reader finds the groove of twist-in-the-tale stories, such often become a-tale-of-the-painfully-obvious.

The trick, then, is to produce an ending the reader isn't expecting, or at least not expecting to such a degree.

An Interesting Day In The Office

Angela paused, mascara brush in hand, to study her reflection. What did Mark see when he gazed so attentively into her eyes? All she saw were the beginnings of crow's feet at their edges. Laughter lines, he'd called them, and he'd made a big thing of moonlight shining in limpid pools, making her smile to prove his point.

'You see,' he'd said, and she'd loved him for it.

Before Mark, laughter had seemed in short supply in her life, or perhaps the sheer grind of a messy divorce had blighted her perspective. But where was her perspective now? What was she doing falling for a man ten years her junior? Or was it nearer fifteen? She'd been loath to ask, but the question kept niggling.

'Why do you need to know?' he'd said. 'We're both adults. Isn't that enough?'

It should have been enough, of course it should, and in normal circumstances Angela knew she'd be able to gloss over their age difference. But they worked together, and the open-plan office was awash with prying eyes and knowing looks and giggling round the coffee station. Giggling at her.

'Bimbos,' he'd said, and the look he'd given her had set her skin alight.

She'd kept him at arm's length, of course she had. After all, this was so *silly*. Yet keeping him at arm's length was silly, too, and if she didn't allow their relationship to blossom she would lose this chance of happiness.

'And I'm not going to,' she told her reflection.

Stepping away, she smoothed the silky fabric of her dress, but there were no wrinkles to smooth. Since Mark had started taking an interest she'd lost weight without even trying, and the dress fitted better now than it had in the shop. The new hairstyle had done wonders, too, the fresh colour making her seem so much more alive that she'd taken the unprecedented step of visiting a beautician. That had been her undoing.

'You've missed a bit with the Polyfilla, Angela. Covering the cracks must be terribly time-consuming.'

Suzanne Marshall had smiled so sweetly after delivering her dig that Angela had thought she'd mis-read the younger woman's intention. Then she realised she hadn't. And then she'd blushed. Suzanne had gaped into her face and laughed aloud. Angela could see it all replaying in the mirror in pastel tones, could see the mouthy bitch moving between the desks telling everyone, and they'd all turned, and they'd all grinned, enjoying her discomfort.

Suzanne now twisted the knife at every opportunity, even to the extent of pouring herself and her low-cut tops over Mark's desk while keeping one eye open for Angela's reaction. Angela hadn't reacted – she hadn't been that stupid – but it still hurt.

Her face was flaming as she thought about it. This was ridiculous. If she was going to dwell on the past it would ruin her future, and she wasn't going to have her future ruined, not by sniggering behind her back, not by caustic digs from any super-bitch. She was going to have a wonderful al fresco meal cooked for her by a sexy man who adored her, and afterwards they would retire for the sort of night she was never going to forget.

Picking up her car keys and the expensive bottle of Chianti, she slammed the door behind her.

She'd never been to Mark's house as he lived so far out on the other side of the city, and they'd always gone on somewhere from work. She'd studied the A Z until the print had nearly faded, but even so, as she passed the end of his street a glance at her wristwatch told her that she was far too early.

She drove round, killing time. The streets were very leafy, nicely kept, so unlike the high-rise where she lived. It had been a gardening magazine that had prompted their first conversation. He'd asked to photocopy an article advertised on the cover and she'd discovered that he had a garden, whereas she had only a balcony and a couple of patio pots. She'd photocopied the article she wanted and had given him the magazine. They'd never looked back.

Angela drove round the block three times, then spied a parking place on his street and took it. She was still early. She tapped the steering wheel; switched on the radio, switched it off again. Without cooling air being forced through the window, she was starting to grow warm. It was going to be a lovely evening. What was the point of sitting cooped up in a car? If Mark was still cooking she could explore his garden.

She rang the bell. She felt conspicuous, standing there, the wine in her hand. The neighbours would be prying. Should she ring the bell again? Perhaps he was in the garden setting the table and hadn't heard her.

She took a side-step to the bay window. There were no net curtains and it was a through room. She could see to what looked like a conservatory, but not to the garden. Beside her the door opened, making her jump.

'Angela! Forgive me, I'm running a bit behind and—'

'I'm early,' she breathed, and she'd never been more pleased.

He was wearing only his bathrobe, his blonde hair dripping water onto the visible 'V' of his naked chest. Water was trickling in rivulets down his powerful calves.

'Oh no...' He backed into the hall at her approach, wagging his finger as if in reprimand while grinning all over his face. 'That's for dessert,' he said. 'In fact, after dessert. I've gone to a lot of trouble to impress you and I'm not having it ruined.'

'You are impressing me,' Angela said, nudging shut the door behind her. 'Impress me some more.'

Juggling the Chianti and her handbag, she playfully reached for the tie to his bathrobe. His smile slipped as he put out a wary arm to forestall her, but he recovered.

'Final word, *no*. At least *not yet*.'

'Spoilsport.' Her pout made him laugh.

'Come on through,' he said.

She was pleased he'd turned his back on her. She could feel a blush beginning. She hadn't meant to come on so strong, hadn't believed she was capable of it. So far theirs had been a true romance – the lingering look, the sensual caress. It had crossed her mind that perhaps he was a virgin, but she'd dismissed that as fantasy on her part. No, doubtless the truth was much more prosaic: someone had hurt him, hurt him terribly. She would never ask. She didn't want the same question asked of her.

The kitchen was heady with aromatic scents, and so warm and steamy that it hid her embarrassment. Mark reached for the extractor's string.

'Knew I should have made a salad.'

'Oh no,' said Angela. 'It smells absolutely wonderful. I'm terribly flattered that you've gone to so much trouble for me.'

He pushed his fingers through his damp hair and then flicked his wrist in an extravagantly theatrical gesture. 'O! It eez noting.'

He escorted her out of the heat of the kitchen and into the conservatory. Bush tomato and capsicum plants stood in pots by the glass, while near the white-washed rear wall cucumber and courgettes climbed out of Gro-bags.

'Good grief,' she breathed. 'I thought you didn't know much about gardening.'

'Ah, this *is* nothing. Come outside and have a look. You'll love it.'

And she did. Beyond the small conservatory was a narrow terrace where he'd set up the table and chairs. Sun-blonded teak, she noted, not stackable patio plastic as on her balcony. Glasses and crockery set on a white damask cloth awaited them, shaded by a square umbrella in pale, starched canvas. It looked beautiful, just as if she'd stepped into the pages of a glossy magazine.

'There's an almond tree at the bottom, go and see. Explore.

Pour the wine, and I'll be back as fast as I can.'

She'd taken a step onto the grass beside the serpentine borders when she heard him shut the conservatory door, a second step when an ominous click resounded in her ears. She paused, telling herself that she'd misheard, but she was drawn back to the terrace, to the conservatory door to test its handle. She hadn't misheard. Mark had locked her out.

She couldn't believe it. What was he doing? Had she upset him? She looked through the glass to the kitchen door. He'd closed that, too. What was he playing at?

From inside the house there was a noise she barely heard, but there was no mistaking the movement of the glass beneath her fingers – an outside door had been opened, and the only other outside door led onto the street.

Side-stepping along the glass, she peered into the through room towards the bay window. She could see no one, but the back of her neck began to prickle.

The glass vibrated again. A door closing.

Angela didn't wait, but flattened herself against the neighbour's wall, into the foliage of a clematis. A head appeared at the bay window, tentatively at first, no more than a silhouette against the sunlight, and then the face came right up to the glass and Angela gasped as Suzanne Marshall shaded her eyes to peer inside the house and beyond, her teeth showing in her triumphant grin.

Angela muffled a cry in her hand. No wonder Mark was running late. She hadn't caught him in the shower. She'd caught him in bed with Suzanne Marshall. Suzanne Marshall had been upstairs all the time, listening to her sexual overture in the hall, laughing herself stupid.

She forced herself to look through the window again, but the younger woman had gone. Pushing by the chairs, Angela ran down the garden. There had to be a way out at the back. She wasn't going to wait to be humiliated again. Where was the rear gate?

There was no rear gate. Angela was trapped. She felt desolate. Tears formed in her eyes. She *had* to get out. The office on Monday would be appalling. The remarks. The innuendos. The giggling at the coffee station. Were they all in on it?

Mark, you bastard! How could you do this to me?

She stared at the fence, looking for a way to climb over it into the neighbouring garden, anything to escape. She didn't care if she skinned her shins or ruined her dress. She'd never wear it again. She hated it, hated herself for being so naïve.

A sob rose in her throat and, as she lifted her head to give it voice, her gaze rested on a spike of deep blue flowers. She knew what they were, knew what they could do, and at that moment she knew that she hated Mark.

The sob was quelled. She wiped her eyes. She blew her nose. She walked back towards the house to stand before the table with its crisp damask cloth and polished cutlery. The bottle opener lay centre stage caught in a spotlight of sunshine. Picking it up, feeling its weight in her hand, Angela turned over possibilities. A victim was only a victim if she allowed herself to be treated like one. And she'd had enough of that. More than enough.

Taking the Chianti by its throat, she pulled its cork and poured a glass. It was very good wine, worth the expense, just as the assistant had promised. For Angela, it was going to be worth its weight in gold.

Retracing her steps down the garden, she took out a tissue to protect her hand and snapped a spike of the deep blue flowers.

Mark appeared as she was fixing her make-up. She smiled at him through the conservatory windows, chuckled when he pretended shock at the locked door.

'Habit,' he explained. 'There are so many burglaries in the area. I can't apologise enough.'

No, she thought, you can't, and she picked up the Chianti to pour him a glass.

'I took to drink in my loneliness. You'll have to catch up.'

He accepted the glass willingly, raising it in salute. 'To us!' he said, and they clinked glasses across the damask cloth with its scattering of tiny, deep blue florets.

The meal started with layers of mozzarella cheese and tomatoes fresh from the conservatory, drizzled with a dressing of olive oil and basil he told her he'd grown himself.

'Very Italian,' she purred. 'Ideal for the Chianti,' and she topped up his glass.

The meal was superb, its taste even out-stripping its teasing aroma. She played the moron when he called it a *Cassoulet Langedoc*, hung onto his every word as he explained it was a bean and pork stew. She laughed at his jokes, coveted his opinions, and kept pouring the wine. He was so full of himself that he didn't realise she was doing no more than wetting her lips with the blood-red liquid. Angela didn't feel like a victim now. She felt like a vampire biding her time.

Her time came when she emptied the bottle into his glass, and he emptied the glass into himself.

'Oops,' he said. 'I'll fetch another.'

She stayed his hand by picking up her glass and throwing the contents onto the lawn.

'No need.' With the base of the glass she grouped the scattered florets. 'I'm sure that will have been quite enough.'

He looked perplexed. Angela waited, knowing that his own conniving guilt would ensure he grasped the truth. He reached out to push at a lone blue floret, so dark as to be almost black against the shroud-like cloth, and she saw his gaze rise to the now empty bottle and then jump to his own empty glass.

'You haven't.' His voice became shrill. 'You can't have! Not these. Angela, you bitch! What the hell were you thinking?'

The 'B' word rang in her head, and she smiled back so sweetly she was surprised her face didn't crack.

'Thinking? Mark, it wasn't my idea. It was Suzanne Marshall's.'

On that final, killing, note, she rose from her seat, picked up her handbag, and in two strides was inside the conservatory locking the door against him. As she walked through the house she could hear him banging on the double glazing. By the time he thought of getting a spade from the shed and putting in the glass, she would be long gone. Then the decision would be his. Did he go to the hospital and tell them he'd been poisoned, or wait it out in his bathroom all night to see if she'd given him only a bit, or had, in fact, been stringing him along?

Serious business, this stringing someone along. And he was still to confront Suzanne Marshall, wasn't he? That would serve her right. It served them both right. Monday was going to be an interesting day in the office.

Commentary

For twist-in-the-tale fiction to be embraced the storyline has to work on an emotional level. Characters have to be believable, readers have to be able to empathise with the characters' predicaments. It is the binding that holds together what are, in truth, some pretty shaky foundations. How does a vulnerable, timid woman, in the space of less than half an hour, change into a confident, calculating, avenging angel?

In truth, she can't. Just as an illusionist dresses himself and his set so as to divert the gaze of his audience from the mechanics of the trick being performed, the writer leads readers away from the obvious by engaging their emotions – in this case engaging a sense of outrage and leading it through to an acceptable form of justice.

The market was a women's magazine and so, for this type of revenge story at least, the main character needed to be female. Third person viewpoint was chosen to give the illusion of close proximity, while in truth keeping readers at arm's length. The joins in the story elements would have been far more noticeable if the narrative had been conveyed in Angela's first person viewpoint. As the magazine was aimed at women in the late 20s-40s age range, I could make Angela an indeterminate older woman, and chose her name accordingly.

For one of the settings I dredged up a personal pet hate: an open-plan office. I've had to work in only one and after the experience vowed never to work in another, though I hasten to add my reasoning was due to the invasive and constant noise, not due to bullying as highlighted in this story.

The third element, the poisonous plant, came from a gardening magazine spotlighting the feature on its cover, along with dining outdoors, which at the time I thought an odd combination, hence it catching my eye. The description of the terrace dining table, the second setting, and of the tiny blue florets from the flower spike, lay in front of me as soon as I opened the magazine; no more research necessary.

Identifying these elements as ingredients for fiction is part of the mindset of a writer. The more we practise coming up with ideas, the more idea elements appear unbidden.

Twist-in-the-tale fiction tends to follow a pre-determined line which rises and falls, akin to a graph. The reader piggy-backs a character bobbling along a straight line, which rises in anticipation, falls in distress, rises in determination and exacts a denouement that is an integral part of the fiction but comes as a surprise to the reader. And this is the form's problem. Telegraph too much and the ending becomes a foregone conclusion that rasps as an anticlimax. Telegraph too little and the reader refuses to believe the ending as given. Reader reaction, important in any type of fiction, takes on an added significance with a twist-in-the-tale story.

At the opening Angela's vulnerability and the reason for it is established in as few words as is necessary, and from this her problem, that she fears her good fortune in hitting it off with Mark too good to be true – which of course it is. This possibility is quickly overlooked by first concentrating on her current sense of wellbeing, then by suffocating both with the memory of Suzanne Marshall's sarcasm and her own discomfort. With an antagonist established, automatically the interrogating spotlight moves away from Mark.

Angela's knowledge of plants is flagged by the exchange of a gardening magazine, her yearning for a better life reflected in the difference in her and Mark's abodes, and the fact that she refers to her gift of wine as *Chianti*, not simply as *red wine*. She wants to live her dream.

All this is conveyed via Angela's eyes, mostly from her memory. In shading a romance between Angela and Mark, Mark needs to be seen in person. His appearance, in a bathrobe, is designed to light both Angela's and readers' expectations, which are mellowed slightly by his reaction to her, yet excused by Angela's mis-reading of the situation. Again, I do not allow readers to dwell on Mark, but divert them by filling Angela's senses first with rich smells of cooking and then by the visual lure of growing vegetables. It is at this point that Angela unwittingly signals Mark's dishonesty ...*I thought you didn't know anything about gardening*... but again it is overlooked by readers as the expensive garden furniture, table setting, and sumptuous garden fill the senses. Mark tells her to pour the wine and...

...and so begins the fall in distress. Angela's descent is taken slowly at first, so that readers catch on to what is happening and are allowed time to race ahead to realise both the magnitude of Mark's betrayal and the devastating effect this will have on vulnerable Angela. She emphasises this by a spurt of pure paranoia when she fears all those working in the open-plan office are a party to the cruelty.

She tries to escape, both from her own embarrassment and the confines of the garden, but already her emotions are turning. She *hates* the dress, *hates* herself for being so naïve – and admits that, *at that moment* she *hates Mark*. The use of the repeated word acts as a braking device in the turmoil, ready for the fall in distress to change to a rise in determination. Taken in these seemingly small steps, readers stand at her shoulder to offer moral support. Even when she recognises the spike of blue flowers for the poison it is, readers will her on to use it.

It is here, too, that the words and phrasing change, in keeping with Angela's subdued emotions, in favour of cold calculation. To emphasise her new-found purpose she takes the Chianti *by its throat* as if she's already enacting her revenge on Mark, and, protecting her hand with a tissue to underscore how potent the florets are, she *snaps* a spike of *deep blue flowers*. The flowers I had in mind, which do exist and for that reason I never name, come in several shades of blue, but deep blue, like the deep red of the Chianti, has connotations I trust readers pick up, though it isn't important if they don't.

When Mark re-enters the story the speed of its delivery is increased, and Angela moves into first person viewpoint for a single, cutting, thought, while she resolutely pours him the wine. With her less rosy view of him, he comes across to readers as arrogant and shallow – *basil he'd grown himself*, referring to a mere bean and pork stew as *Cassoulet Langedoc* – and as he had led her on, so she leads him on, while she keeps pouring the wine, which becomes *blood-red* and she *a vampire biding her time*.

When it is Mark's turn to realise something is wrong, the delivery is again slowed and individual words are chosen with care: *push at a lone blue floret, so dark as to be almost black against the shroud-like cloth...*

This, in itself, is not a twist for readers, as readers have been waiting for Mark's realisation to dawn so as to be able to harvest a fairly natural, if somewhat dubious, emotional reaction: that he'd been poisoned and "deserved" to be. The given twist is not that he and Suzanne Marshall plotted against Angela, but that Angela and Suzanne Marshall had plotted against him.

This is the twist designed to draw readers up short. And while they try to fathom how they missed it, Angela lets it be known that, as Mark had her, she had been *stringing him along* – and by definition, readers, as well.

Readers never see Angela adding the florets to the bottle, but that is the inference I wanted them to grasp – an inference that wouldn't have worked as smoothly if the story had been conveyed in the closer proximity of first person viewpoint. Did Angela poison the wine? Or did Angela just imply that she'd poisoned the wine?

Whichever, when he is able it will be human nature for Mark to question Suzanne Marshall, thus souring their relationship, which they won't be able to make public for fear of censure from other members of the office staff, leaving Angela quietly triumphant.

A twist upon a twist upon a twist.

Over To You

Twist-in-the-tale stories are difficult to write well, but that doesn't make them impossible to write. Read as many as you can to gain a feel for what works, and bear in mind that a twist-in-the-tale storyline can be overlaid on any genre.

My suggestion to aid writing your own is to pull together two or three elements and tumble them through *what if..?* so as to create a straight storyline that has an acceptable ending. Study the ending. How can it be subverted? Can characters' roles be reversed? List possibilities and again tumble these through *what if..?* until a twist catches your attention. Then work backwards in the plotting steps to a feasible start and groom your characters to behave believably within the confines of the plotting steps. Choice of words and phrases can help create misdirection for readers, so pay attention to the details.

An Introduction To

Turning Back The Clock

This story was written specifically for a market aimed at the female 20s-30s age range. The magazine insisted on easy-reading first-person viewpoint stories, and if the submission had a romance element it had more chance of being accepted. However, a sex scene, or a love scene, even a fast grope scene, would not only see the typescript winging back, but scribbled across the top would be *Don't waste my time*.

Editors keep a note of writers who waste their time, just as they keep a note of writers who show promise. It can mean the difference between a story being assessed immediately or returned after a quick glance at the initial page. Editors are professionals and they expect writers to be, too. This means studying a market before submitting to it.

Turning Back The Clock

London was just as I remembered it: big, bustling, raucous and filthy. Why anyone would possibly want to move south to live and work in the place was beyond me. The sooner I could get back on the train the better.

Of course, my view might have been rather more rosy if my conversation with the publisher's editor had gone more along the lines I'd imagined.

I'd been writing to the woman for months, trying to alter my typescript on her advice so that it would be acceptable to her employers. When she had asked me to come down for a meeting I'd been over the moon, thinking that it meant I'd hit the formula at last. But it had all been a complete waste of time. She didn't say a single thing that couldn't have been written in an email or discussed on the phone. She'd shown more interest in my accent than in my novel.

I'd climbed out of bed at five that morning to catch the train, and I'd been in her office exactly thirty-five minutes. To say that I was disappointed was putting it mildly. On my way out of the building I'd stepped into the ladies to shed a few discreet tears of frustration, touch up my mascara and comb my hair. Life would go on, I told myself. What I needed at that moment was to go somewhere quiet for a coffee while I reassessed my situation.

Leaving my security tag on the reception desk, I walked through the automatic glass doors to the marbled steps beyond, and winced as the traffic noise assaulted my eardrums. People pushed past me as they left or entered the building; they seemed to have no time to be polite. Time meant money. Life was too short.

I looked up and down the street, wondering which way to go.

I wasn't sure if I had either the energy or the determination to force myself along the pavement with the other hurrying people. Perhaps it would be better to take the Tube and head straight for King's Cross.

'Zoe..?'

I heard my name, but the caller couldn't mean me. In London no one knew me. There wasn't anybody I could casually run into.

'Zoe?' It was a man's voice, a voice with a deep resonant tone, and this time it sounded more confident. Perhaps it was me he was calling. After all, how many Zoes could there be within earshot?

I turned as he touched my arm, and looked up into a pair of lustrous hazel eyes.

'It is Zoe, isn't it?'

His name eluded me for a moment, but I'd looked into those eyes before, looked and longed and loved, many years ago.

Adam, Adam Hunt. And I was seventeen again, walking from the youth club to the bus station wrapped in his warm, protective arms.

I blinked myself back to the present, but my heart continued to pound as I took in his expensive suit and stylishly cut hair. Adam had always had style, even when he'd worn jeans. That indefinable poise of his, together with his fine bone structure and pale complexion, had lifted him above the rest. He'd always been devilishly attractive.

'Hello, Adam,' I said.

'You remember me!' He opened his arms in amazement, letting a grin crease his face from ear to ear and light up his eyes. Those eyes – magnetic, they were, hypnotic. I was unsure of what my racing pulse was telling me.

'I'm surprised you recognised me,' I began. 'It's been a long time.'

'Nonsense,' he said. 'You haven't changed a bit.'

I smiled at the compliment, even though I knew it was an

exaggeration. I'd added a stone to my skinny frame since I'd last set eyes on Adam – marriage and two children had seen to that.

Our conversation faltered. We stood on the steps of the office block, the noise of London battering at us from all sides, and we looked at each other. Was he remembering the past, too? Was he reliving the moonlit strolls, the softly whispered declarations of love; his demanding lips on mine?

I changed my line of thought, determined to speak brightly of the weather, or his job, of anything neutral, but it was Adam who spoke first.

'So what are you doing in London? Not living here, surely? Wide open spaces were more to your liking, if I remember correctly.'

I turned my gaze aside, blushing slightly at his clear memory of me. Maybe I'd meant more to him than I'd believed, perhaps as much as he had meant to me.

'No,' I answered, 'just visiting.'

'Still writing those stories of yours? Those romances?'

His tone changed before he'd finished speaking, his eyes growing wide as he pointed to the building behind me.

'You've been here!' he exclaimed. 'You're a novelist!'

I groaned inside and tried to make light of it. It would have been lovely to have been able to say yes, to have bubbled with excitement, to have shared it all with him; but there was no point kidding myself. I hadn't made it, and at that moment I felt I never would.

'Not exactly,' I replied, 'but I keep trying.'

His face clouded a little and he relaxed his stance in sympathy. 'You've had a disappointment. I can tell.'

I longed to step across to him and let him hold me close, the way he used to when I was a teenager and felt that life had let me down.

'This is ridiculous,' he said, 'the pair of us shouting above the traffic. Have you time for a coffee?'

The thought cheered me. 'I'd been considering that when I

saw you. It's an awfully long time since breakfast.'

He glanced at his watch and slipped an arm round my back, sending a tingle up my spine.

'Good idea. How about lunch instead?'

I was so surprised I hadn't the good manners to accept graciously. 'Have you the time? Aren't you working?'

He waved away my reservations and guided me through the bustling throng on the pavement.

'No problem. I know just the place.'

He hailed a taxi as if he'd been doing it all his life, and we were whisked away to I knew not where. I didn't care, either. The burden of responsibility had been taken from my shoulders and I wouldn't have to think, or consider, or decide for a whole hour. Adam would do it all, just as he had when we were young and I was shy and unsure of myself. He cared. He had time for my feelings, time for conversation.

How different from Richard.

It hadn't been Richard's fault, not in the beginning. He'd been so desperate to have his own business, be his own man, as he called it. If it had made him happy I wouldn't have minded hardly ever seeing him, but it didn't. He'd become quick-tempered and moody, without a good word for either of the girls. And every time I picked up a pen there'd be a stream of sarcastic remarks about the many rejections my stories were collecting.

Where are the sales, Zoe? Where's the money?

I should have known the business wasn't doing well, but Richard would never discuss it. When I realised to what extent we were in debt it was far too late. Richard vowed to repay every creditor, and he managed to get a job with another contractor. He worked days, and I worked evenings, but I resented the way my life had changed, resented the way time to write had been denied me. Most of all I resented the way Richard derided my efforts as fruitless.

Adam wouldn't have done that, I felt sure. Adam would have

understood. He'd been the first person I'd shown my stories to. He hadn't laughed; he'd encouraged me.

I'd expected to be taken to lunch at a wine bar, or a restaurant, but instead we pulled up outside a chic hotel. A dignified waiter led us to a secluded table by a little grotto with a lily pond. I glanced in as we passed and was enchanted to see that there were carp swimming in the softly gurgling waters.

The waiter took my coat and eased me into a padded rattan chair, then he gave us both the menu and wine list. I daren't open either for fear of the prices I'd see. Instead I gazed at the exotic decor.

'Do you come here often?' I asked, and I blushed as I realised what I'd said. Adam took it in good part, though, and we both laughed. It seemed to break the ice.

'Only with clients,' he told me, lowering his head in mock conspiracy. 'You're a client, Zoe, then this can go on my expense account.'

We laughed again, and I felt much better.

With his guidance, we ordered. Our starter arrived almost at once. This place obviously had a name for its service.

'Actually,' Adam said, 'the little lie about your being a client might not be as far fetched as you might think. You see, I'm in the publishing business myself.'

'You're not!'

'Yes,' he said, 'and it's due, in part, to you. Remember those stories you typed for me?'

I nodded, but it was a time I'd rather forget, a time just before we split up.

Adam grinned. 'Well, I never did sell them. In fact I never sold ninety per cent of my fiction, but I visited plenty of publishing houses, and I soon realised that my talents would be better employed on their side of the fence. So here I am – a publishing executive.'

He took a long look at me and then reached across the table

to take my hand, squeezing it gently.

'It's so good to see you again, Zoe. You really don't know how good.'

The sincerity in his voice touched me, and we sat there a moment smiling at each other. I knew he, too, was remembering the past. But the waiter returned, and the spell was broken.

'Well, never mind about me,' Adam began in a lighter vein, 'tell me about yourself. How are you? What have you been doing? I see you're married now.'

Absently I fingered my wedding ring. So he'd noticed. I wondered when: before or after he'd asked me to lunch.

'Yes,' I said. 'Seven years.'

Looking across at Adam, I didn't know how it could possibly be so long. It seemed only yesterday that Adam and I were shrieking our delight high up on the ferris wheel at the local fair.

'Happy, are you?'

It was a question I'd not expected.

'Yes,' I said, but I took rather too long to answer him and everything but the word said No.

I could lie to myself, force myself to believe that my marriage would miraculously regain its former lustre, but I could not lie to Adam.

'We're having problems – financial,' I added quickly, 'cash-flow, the recession. My husband's a builder.' I was fudging and it was obvious. I wished I'd said nothing at all.

Adam nodded sympathetically.

A faint depression hung over the table, lengthening our pause into an uncomfortable silence. I longed to ask him if he was married – he wasn't wearing a ring – but I couldn't find the courage. Perhaps I didn't want to know.

'I'm a mother, too,' I said, smiling with the pride I truly felt.

Adam looked astonished. 'Never!'

'Yes, they're five and four, and—'

'—and the image of their mother,' Adam cut across me.

I blushed a little. Both took after their father, but I didn't tell Adam. I liked the way he had with words, turning every phrase into a compliment, restoring my battered self-esteem. It seemed churlish to correct him.

We drank our wine and he told me a little about his job. Had it been anyone else I would have questioned him closely for the coveted information that might have helped me find an acceptance for my novel, but the book was far from my mind. I just wanted to sit and listen to the rich timbre of his voice, be soothed by his charm, enchanted by his mystique.

After dessert, Adam suggested we take coffee in the lounge. Gallantly, he helped me from my seat – something Richard would never have thought of doing – and he placed an arm lightly about my waist drawing me close. My every muscle tensed in anticipation. In my youth Adam had awakened the first true stirrings of womanhood within me, now he lit the flames of passionate desire.

'It's a pity it's not Friday,' he said, pointing to the deserted dance floor. 'They have a quartet. I could have held you in my arms the way I did when we were both young and innocent.'

He smiled at me with his eyes, but I looked away, afraid he would read my thoughts.

We sat on a long, cushioned seat, our coffee on a table before us, for all the world the only two people alive in London. Adam stretched a little and draped an arm round my shoulder. He gave me a little hug and I could feel myself melting into the curve of his body.

'It really is good to see you, Zoe,' he murmured. 'A friendly face amid the rushing tide. It makes a man believe again.'

The catch in his voice told me that his protective shell held a chink. My heart went out to him. 'Is life not treating you well?'

He chuckled, embarrassed, I think, that I should be able to see his inner feelings.

'Oh, life's all right. Materially, I couldn't ask for more.'

He paused, and I knew then that he yearned for times past.

'You know what it's like, Zoe. You've always hated the cities. And the business doesn't help. It's all trite one-liners and double-talk.'

He seemed lost in his thoughts for a moment, then he looked at me as if for the first time, and he smiled, not just with his lips, but with his whole being. I could feel myself glowing; I couldn't help it.

'Zoe, I was a fool to let you go. I didn't know what I had.'

I didn't know how to answer him, I wasn't sure of how I should feel. He eased my head on to his shoulder. I didn't resist.

'We were young,' I murmured.

'Yes,' he agreed, 'we were.'

I felt his fingertip softly trace a pattern on my cheek. I closed my eyes and let my senses float. It was like falling in love all over again.

'But we're older now,' he breathed. 'We know what we want, what we have to offer. We could pick up where we left off.'

I opened my eyes and smiled to myself. Adam was trying to seduce me, just as he had when I'd been seventeen and too unsure of myself to venture down his path. All the same, I was flattered.

'I'm only here for the day,' I said, trying to make light of it.

'Well... this is a hotel...'

The sense of flattery evaporated.

Yes, it was a hotel. Had that been the reason for Adam bringing me here? Had it been in his mind when he'd first seen me?

We know what we want, what we have to offer...

Adam had always known what he wanted, what he had to offer, that was the trouble. He wasn't offering me a loving affair now, not even a one-night stand. He was offering me an hour of passion in a hotel bedroom which his employers would pay for by way of an expense account. I felt cheapened.

I knew I shouldn't be. Adam had spoken of trite one-liners

and double-talk, yet what was it but a description of himself. He'd not changed from the silver-tongued Lothario I'd been so infatuated with nine years before. There had been rumours of his conquests and I'd denied the truth of them, seeing only what I wanted. Days before my eighteenth birthday he'd tossed me aside without a qualm.

No, Adam had not changed. More to the point, neither had I. I still only saw what I wanted. It was about time I grew up.

Lifting my head from his shoulder, I smiled up into his expectant eyes as I untwined myself from his arms.

'You can't recapture the past,' I said.

His expression changed fractionally, but the twinkle in his eyes was soon restored.

'Perhaps not,' he conceded, 'but it was good to see you again, anyway.'

'Yes,' I replied. 'It was good to see you, too.'

I rose to collect my coat from the rack, aware of his penetrating gaze on my every movement. I tried, but I couldn't walk out of the hotel without one last look at him, one last look at my wooer, my desire.

He raised his fingers in a little wave and shot me a smile that would have melted gold.

I walked through the doors into the noisy street knowing that I was in love with Adam, that I had been in love with him ever since I'd been seventeen and he had swept my off my feet with his charm.

But I'm older now, my sight clearer. The Adam I love is an illusion, part man, part imagination, too delicate to be tainted by the constrictions of reality.

I must admit, I prefer it that way. It's much more romantic.

Commentary

Okay, I'll own up: a northern writer travelling south at the behest of a London publisher to be met with rejection, a suave ex boyfriend ready to take up where he left off... how much of this is autobiographical? Not as much as you are imagining.

Yes, I was invited to a London publishing house, and I did have to get up at the crack of dawn to make the meeting, and the editor did only want to look me up and down, much to my chagrin; there was also a suave ex boyfriend, older in mentality than his years, and he did write fiction, but the two were separate incidents in my life. This, though, is the epitome of the advice "write about what you know".

Once these elements were fictionalised it was simple to exchange my financially sound, supportive husband for... Originally the husband character was a thoroughly bad lot, but I toned him down and gave him reasons for acting the way he does, so as to make him come over as a normal, shades-of-grey person reacting not-too-well to problems in his life.

The big difference lays in the temperaments of Zoe and me. She's a fluffy-bunny sort of person, rose-tinted spectacles and all, whereas I am far more down to earth. She's not me, but I had to become her so as to convincingly convey her somewhat childish view of life. She is, at heart, a true romantic, living in a world where the sun shines every day, fairy godmothers do exist, and somewhere over the rainbow...

After *Permanently Portugal* and *An Interesting Day At The Office*, this story has doubtless read saccharine sweet, but the point I'm making in its choice here is that although the previous two stories were aimed at women's magazines, as was this one, they weren't aimed at the same women's magazines. The elements and tone of *Turning Back The Clock* were designed to fit not just the market's stated parameters, but the overall tone of the magazine, including its Readers' Letters, its non-fiction features, and its advertisements. It is being able to do this that separates a hobby writer, who first writes fiction and then looks for a market, from a professional who writes fiction targeted at a specific market.

Having decided on the characters and the tone, how is the story placed on the page? By choosing words carefully, right from the start. *London was big, bustling, raucous and filthy.* People from all over the world have an image of London. *Big* and *bustling* merge well enough with whatever image is held, and the words were chosen for their alliteration. *Raucous* is a questionable fit; *filthy* is designed to set readers back on their heels, to grab their attention. I then feed in a dream carried by many readers, to have a book published, and immediately dash the dream, setting up a strand of empathy. I intimate how other people can be uncaring of an individual seemingly lost in a maelstrom, and bring in what amounts to a knight in shining armour to carry Zoe, if not on a white charger at least in a hailed cab, to a place of luxurious safety where she is the focus of his adoring attention.

Written in this story-board form, Zoe sounds a bit of a self-obsessed wimp, but I use sensual description to create a softer focus. While she's on her own the word images I create are hard: *automatic glass doors, marbled steps, winced as the traffic noise assaulted...* When Adam comes into the story the images become more languid by the use of double adjectives: *deep resonant tone, lustrous hazel eyes.* I slow the reader further using alliterative, rhythmic phrasing *I'd looked into those eyes before, looked and longed and loved, many years ago.* This helps in conveying the anticipation that she's going to be swept off her feet, and readers are there, voyeuristically sharing her emotions.

It is anticipation that makes this story work, not the depth of its characterisation or its content. It is anticipation that makes most genre fiction work for readers, and that means the writer paying particularly attention to pacing.

Zoe's home-life is not given in a single block of paragraphing, and neither is her past relationship with Adam. Each is drip-fed into the moving stream of their on-going conversation, sometimes acting as a spur, sometimes as a warning. Even the dialogue tags are placed with care in order to create an effective pause in delivery. Zoe has been married seven years, the stereotypical inference readers take being that she's ripe for an affair. Adam shares his name with the First Man in the Garden of Eden. Subliminal it might be, but details such as these matter. They coax the reader along.

When Adam cuts across Zoe as she's trying to explain about her children, she takes it as a mis-placed compliment, whereas readers flag it that he is deliberately deflecting the conversation. From then on, if not before, readers are waiting for him to make his move, waiting to see exactly what his move will be, and how Zoe will respond. They know that *The catch in his voice told me that his protective shell held a chink* holds nothing of the kind, and that she's taken his bait. It is at this point, as Adam is reeling in Zoe, I am reeling in the reader, ready to shower both with a little cold reality. But only a little. This is a romance, and that means readers of the magazine are looking for an upbeat, satisfying ending so they can leave the story with a sigh or a smile, preferably with both.

Zoe internalises that, like Adam, she hasn't changed, and she doesn't change even at the end of the story. She remains a true romantic at heart, rose-tinted spectacles firmly in place.

Over To You

So, a first person viewpoint story with an element of romance but no overt sex... It's not as easy as it sounds, but this is your mission.

Choose an incident from your life; think back to an old flame. How could the two be integrated? Muse on both for a while to allow the separate memories to rise to the surface. Re-live them a little. Think of each in terms of the five senses: sight, touch, hearing, smell, taste. Toss in *what if..?* and list possibilities until one grabs your attention.

And remember, for you, it doesn't have to be a female viewpoint, or even a human viewpoint.

Mining your own past this way can provide fertile ground for fiction. Just don't stick to the truth as it happened. Slip on your rose-tinted spectacles and write the truth as it might have been.

An Introduction To

Jeremy

In the final example of Women's Fiction, variations in the female view have been set aside for that of family members.

The wider family, their trials and tribulations, is fertile ground for fiction aimed at women, especially the 30-50 age range juggling work, home and child rearing. Unlike the narrower aspects of Self, this sub-genre has always been used to explore social issues that impinge on readers' lives.

The target magazine took longer stories on occasion, particularly if their emotional content was high. As ever when writing for a market, it pays to submit what its editor seeks.

Jeremy

'I wouldn't ask if it wasn't an emergency.'

Megan was taking on her mother's tone, Frank could hear it rising in his daughter's voice.

'I mean, it's not as if you've anything else to do.'

'You don't know what I've got to do,' he countered.

'I know what you don't do. You don't go bowling anymore, you don't go fishing, and you're certainly incapable of using your own washer.'

To sharpen her point, Megan lifted his freshly ironed laundry from her basket and dropped it on the chair beside him. Frank winced.

'Who else am I going to leave him with?' she continued. 'You'd prefer that I ask some stranger off the street? Good grief, Dad, I've got to go out to work and he is your only grandchild.'

Frank winced again, this time shooting a surreptitious glance at Sean. As usual he was bent over the tiny screen of his electronic game – *beep, beep, ping, zap, beep* – and wasn't taking a blind bit of notice of the conversation. A good job, too, Frank reckoned. It wasn't going very well.

'It'll only be for a few days, a week at the most, until I can make other arrangements,' Megan said.

Frank realised he had to say something before he gave in by default.

'It's a parent's responsibility—'

'Don't start that. Do you think I like working these hours and leaving Sean with a childminder before and after school? Or are you suggesting that the poor woman should have given a fortnight's notice to have appendicitis?'

'All right, all right. For a week, just a week.'

Again he looked at the small blond head, eyes staring,

thumbs moving faster than Frank could comprehend. *Beep, beep, ping, zap, beep.* How on earth was he going to cope with this for a week?

Frank was awake with the dawn chorus, fretting about the coming day. Sean had been lovely as a baby. He'd pushed him in the park and they'd fed the ducks together. He'd become argumentative as a toddler, when his father had left. Nursery hadn't seemed to help, and then there had been all that to-ing and fro-ing to the hospital before June had died and... well... somehow he'd turned into a sullen schoolchild glued to a piece of beeping plastic.

He wished June was here. June could charm the birds from the trees. She would have known how to separate Sean from that noisy contraption and hold a conversation. But what sort of a conversation do you have with a six year old? June would have known. Frank hadn't a clue.

When they arrived Megan was a different person.

'I'm sorry about yesterday, Dad. I shouldn't have become so heated.'

'That's okay, love.' He wanted to say that he was sorry, too, that he should have offered to help immediately, his only daughter, his only grandchild, but the words wouldn't come, and then Sean sidled by, a pale and silent wraith in his drab school uniform.

'I've made you both a cake,' Megan said, handing Frank a foil-wrapped plate. You can have it for your tea. Be a good boy, Sean, and do what your grandad says. I'll see you tonight.'

Dropping the latch behind her, Frank turned towards the kitchen-diner, but even before he was halfway down the hall the sounds were echoing up to meet him. *Beep, beep, ping, zap, beep.*

He entered the kitchen with a sense of trepidation. Just as he'd expected, Sean was leaning over his game, his thumbs moving faster than light. *Beep, beep, ping, zap, beep.* Frank placed the cake on the counter, surprised to realise that his hand was trembling.

'Do— do you want breakfast?' he asked.

The small head shook, its blonde hair rising in a cloud. *Beep, beep, ping, zap, beep.*

'Can I make you a drink, then?'

Sean's head shook again, but his eyes never lifted from the tiny screen. *Beep, beep, ping, zap, beep.*

Frank made his own breakfast, slowly to fill the time, but it tasted like cardboard, his tea like washing-up water.

'Can I watch television?' Sean asked.

'Er, yes. Yes, of course. Shall I...?'

Frank started to rise, but Sean had already left the kitchen, and a moment later Frank could hear the television in the lounge. *Vroom-vroom, rat-a-tat-tat, argh!!* Sean was sitting cross-legged on the rug, his gaze locked on the larger screen, the bright flashing colours of the cartoon and its all-pervading noise blocking out rational thought. *Rat-a-tat-tat. Aargh!! Vroom-vrooooooom!*

It was a relief when the alarm sounded on Sean's wristwatch and, without being told, he pulled on his coat for school and headed for the door.

'Do you want me to walk with you?' Frank asked, unable to think of anything else to say.

Sean shook his head.

'See you tonight, then.' And for the first time his grandson nodded.

It was the same in the late afternoon, except in reverse.

'What did you do at school?' Frank asked.

'Nothing much,' replied Sean, and the television was switched on for the noisy cartoons. When the news started, the electronic gadget was pulled from his bag and the air filled with *beep, beep, ping, zap, beep* until Frank called him for his beans on toast and his piece of chocolate cake. They were eaten in a silence Frank didn't know how to break. And then the game started again, and the noises. *Beep, beep, ping, zap, beep.* By the time Megan arrived after work, Frank felt as if he'd done fourteen hours hard labour. Megan was grateful, and talkative, but all Frank wanted to do was close the door behind them and flop exhausted into a chair.

It was the same the next day. And the morning after that. Dropping the latch behind Sean, Frank went into the living room to stand by the window and watch the boy start for school. He walked purposefully, not dragging his heels or kicking at crisp packets blowing in the breeze the way some of the other children did who passed Frank's gate. Other children did pass, but they didn't look at Sean, and Sean didn't look at them. It was if they weren't walking in the same street.

Frank let the net curtain fall and turned back to the kitchen and his cooling tea. He should be able to do this, take care of his grandson, but he couldn't. He couldn't cope, not with the noise, not with the silences. Megan must have friends, women of her own age, who were used to children. There had to be someone who could look after Sean instead of him. But how to tell Megan? She'd fly off the handle, and he wouldn't be able to cope with that, either.

He sat at the table, in front of his cold tea and his unopened newspaper, watching the spring sunshine trail shadows across the Formica. The hammering on the door was so unexpected that he slopped his tea into the saucer. He was still bleary-eyed when he stared at a dishevelled Sean panting on the doorstep.

'Grandad! Grandad!'

There didn't seem to be any more explanation so Frank ushered him inside, glancing at the hall clock on the way into the kitchen. It was just gone eleven. Why wasn't he in school?

In the kitchen it all came out in a rush.

'Mark Thomas... It'll die! ...so cold. ...needs our help. Grandad, we have to do something!'

Trying to calm him, Frank realised that his little hands were cupped one on top of the other. A mouse, Frank thought. Sean had brought home one of the pet mice from school. There'd be hell to pay now, from every side. From the school, from Megan...

Sean lifted one grubby hand to reveal a baby bird stretched out on his palm, only two fawn downies attached to its translucent, purple-hued skin, its little heart faintly visible beneath and pumping for all it was worth. The chick's improbably longs legs were stretched out to Sean's wrist, its huge yellow-edged beak lying on his fingers. Its eyes were closed and it didn't look as if they were about to open.

'We found it at playtime, under the hedge. It fell out of its nest. We couldn't find it. Mark Thomas tried to stamp on it.' Sean's lower lip trembled. 'I hit him.'

'Good,' said Frank, without thinking.

Sean's eyes were beginning to well. 'I took it to Miss Jacobs. She said I had to put it back and let its parents look after it.' He turned his little face to Frank as a tear streamed down his cheek.

'But they can't, Grandad. How can they lift him back into the nest? He'll die of cold. Feel him.'

Sean lifted his hand and Frank touched the scrawny thing with a fingertip. It did feel very cold. It felt close to death. He looked at Sean and wondered how on earth he was going to cope with that.

'Sean, it's—'

'He needs warmth, like he was back in his nest. And he needs feeding. We've got to feed him, Grandad, and keep him warm!'

Sean closed his free hand over the chick again, hugging it to his body. 'What do we do, Grandad?' The little face looked up, eyes imploring.

'Do..?' murmured Frank. He gulped, glancing at Sean's cupped hands before returning to the boy's face.

But his grandson's expression had become a mask, his eyes shielded, his emotions locked away, and Frank felt a terrible pressure build in his chest. Mark Thomas had tried to kill the chick, Miss Jacobs had dismissed it, and now, he, Sean's only grandfather…

Frank straightened his shoulders and cleared his throat. 'We keep it warm,' he stated. 'And to keep it warm, we… er…' He lifted a finger in the air as the idea came to him. 'We use a hot water bottle!'

Leaving Sean in the kitchen, he scurried upstairs to retrieve the hot water bottle he'd kicked out of bed that morning. His heart was beating quite hard by the time he returned, and his breathing was a little ragged, but the pressure in his chest had vanished. Sean watched as he filled the kettle, his eyes still wary. Frank pretended not to notice.

'Right,' he said. 'Now a nest. How about a small bowl? That's nest-shaped, isn't it?'

Sean's mouth opened in a gasp, and he turned to pull at the door of Frank's crockery cupboard. A plastic bowl was chosen and placed on top of the filled hot water bottle.

'Yes,' said Frank, testing the temperature of the plastic. 'That's warming up nicely.'

'We can line it with kitchen roll to make it soft,' Sean said, his eyes shining now.

'Good thinking!'

In no time at all the nest was made and the chick laid into it, bright yellow beak leaning upright against the side. Frank and Sean stood together peering at the bird. It didn't seem to be breathing, but its little heart was pumping rapidly.

'He'll be thirsty,' said Sean

'Yes,' murmured Frank.

'And hungry,' said Sean.

Frank pursed his lips. This was going to be a bit more tricky.

They tried giving the chick a drink of water from an egg-spoon, but the bird was too weak to hold up its head and the water dribbled down its body. Frank thought it might be unconscious, but didn't like to mention this to Sean.

'We have to make him open his beak,' said Sean frowning hard at the bird.

'Make it..?' said Frank in alarm. 'But we could do it serious injury.' He pushed out his hands to show how big they were in comparison to the chick.

It was Sean who picked up the bird, nestling it in his palm, holding up its yellow beak between his thumb and index finger. 'Mum presses my cheeks when I won't take medicine. Come on, Jeremy, open your beak.'

'*Jeremy?*' Frank said.

Sean wouldn't raise his eyes from the chick and his voice dropped to a whisper. 'If he's got a name he won't die.'

'Ah... yes...' mused Frank, trying to come to terms with the enormity of Sean's commitment. 'Well, Jeremy is a good name.'

Sean concentrated and, with the merest squeeze, the yellow beak opened a fraction. Frank emptied the egg-spoon of water down Jeremy's throat.

'He swallowed it, Grandad!'

'Yes,' he said, feeling a glow radiating through him. 'Yes, he did, didn't he?'

'We need worms, Grandad. Birds eat worms.'

They left Jeremy in his warm plastic nest and scouted the garden for worms. It took twenty minutes to find one, but it was so big it could have eaten Jeremy. Sean was becoming desperate.

'Do you have any worms?' he asked the lady next door as she hung out her washing.

Frank groaned. Mrs Bexton was a gossip and, just as Frank expected, she wanted to know the far end of everything.

'Jeremy, eh?' She eyed Frank before refocusing her attention on Sean. 'You don't want worms,' she told him. 'Cat food's the thing, mixed with a bit of water.'

Much to Frank's surprise, and Sean's delight, she brought out some of her cat's meat on a saucer.

'Little and often,' she warned. 'You're not stuffing a turkey.'

They tried the mixture from the tip of the egg-spoon, but tweezers proved more successful. Jeremy soon got the idea and swallowed on cue.

'He's got a tongue,' whispered Sean. 'I can see it moving.'

When Jeremy strained and produced a bag of faeces, Sean was mesmerised.

'Ah,' said Frank. 'I think young Jeremy needs a nappy.'

'Birds don't have nappies,' Sean chided. 'I've seen it on nature programmes on the television. They do this so that the mother bird can clean the nest when she's fed the chicks.'

'All I can say is it's a good job we're only caring for one, and not six.'

The phone started ringing and Frank left Sean feeding Jeremy. Megan was on the other end of the line. She was incandescent.

'Why didn't you ring the school when he turned up?' she demanded. 'They've called the childminder, they've called me, they've just about got the police out searching for him!'

Frank made placating noises and promised to have Sean back at school for the afternoon session. Sean didn't want to go, and when Frank said he'd walk with him to explain to Miss Jacobs, Sean fretted that Jeremy would die without someone to look after him.

'He'll die without food,' said Frank, 'and the way he's eating this we'll run out by tonight, so we'll need to go shopping for him. And I'll be ever so quick,' Frank promised.

Sean took him at his word and kept hurrying him all the way to school. Miss Jacobs was very understanding when everything was explained to her, and said she'd find books on the life cycle of birds for the class to look at.

As Frank was coming out of the supermarket with a packet of kitten food, his eye was caught by a familiar shop on the opposite pavement, and Jeremy's future rolled out before him. Crossing the road, Frank wondered why he hadn't thought of it before.

*

Sean must have sprouted wings and flown to Frank's house after school, he arrived so quickly, dumping his bag and his coat in a heap in the hall in his rush to the kitchen. When he saw Jeremy, his relief was palpable.

'He's all right.'

'Of course he's all right,' said Frank. 'Do you think that I'm incapable? There's a present for him in the fridge, in a tin. Don't spill it.'

Sean went to investigate, crying out in disbelief when he saw the wriggling mass of white grubs.

'Maggots! Oh Grandad, that's wonderful. Miss Jacobs got us a book and it said that was what birds eat.'

'Well, that and other things,' said Frank. 'I thought it would help with the cat food. They'll certainly be better to pick up with tweezers. Shall we see if Jeremy likes them?'

Jeremy liked the maggots, but Megan wasn't so keen.

'You've got *what* in your fridge?' she said when she came in.

Sean and Frank stood, a united front in protection of Jeremy's diet. Megan relented.

'Just so long as Jeremy, and Jeremy's maggots, stay here.'

Sean was crestfallen. 'But Mum...'

'Of course he's stopping here,' Frank said, eyeing Sean. 'We can't risk him catching a chill, or being frightened by the journey, can we?' Sean thought it through and nodded.

'You will look after him until I get back in the morning, won't you, Grandad?'

It had been a long day. Frank had promised that he would guard Jeremy, and guard Jeremy he would. He cleared the bedside table and brought the hot water bottle and the plastic nest to sit beside his bed, then he switched out the light. Something was nagging at the back of Frank's mind, and for a while he wasn't sure what it was. Then he realised. There had been no noisy cartoons on the television, and no beeping electronic game.

*

Frank had been feeding Jeremy for an hour when Sean arrived the next morning to take over. He didn't say anything, but stood close by as Sean reached into the plastic nest to take hold of the chick.

'Grandad! He's opened his eyes. Jeremy looked at me!'

'Did he now?' Frank ruffled his grandson's hair, and gave Megan a wink. Shaking her head in disbelief, she left for work.

Between the cat food and the maggots, Jeremy flourished. By the end of that second day he was cheeping faintly. By the end of the third day, his eyes were fully open and his legs were scrabbling for purchase. By the end of the fourth day Sean had a trick to show.

'Look at this, Mum.'

He tapped sharply on the edge of the plastic nest and Jeremy struggled upright, his bright beak open and demanding. Sean fed him two maggots which were swallowed whole.

'Voracious, isn't he?' she said.

'You can say that again,' agreed Frank. 'Feeding every fifteen minutes... I have new respect for our feathered friends outside.'

Megan took her father's arm and hugged him. 'And you look tired.'

'Oh I'm all right. Better than I've felt for ages, actually. It's doing Sean good, too.' He bent closer to his daughter. 'Not a sign of that confounded noisy gadget of his.'

'Mmm, but it's a *wild* bird, Dad. It's not a pet. And it's going to grow feathers and fly.'

Smiling, Sean turned to them. 'Jeremy's nestling up to me like I'm his mummy.'

'Yes,' said Megan, 'I can see that,' and she looked pointedly at Frank.

Over the next week Jeremy did start to grow feathers, first sky-blue quills on his skinny wings and then a burst of tiny, inky-black plumage. Sean and Frank studied bird books borrowed from the library.

'I think Jeremy is a starling,' said Sean.

'I think he's a blackbird,' said Frank.

Jeremy ate, and he grew, and he chirruped, and finally he hopped out of his plastic nest all by himself.

'Aw! Wicked!' said Sean, but Frank knew that it was time to talk of Jeremy's future.

'But why can't he stay with us?' Sean pleaded. 'He's my friend.'

'I know he is, but soon he'll be ready to live outside, and you can't talk to him like a mother bird can. You can't tell him that he's got to watch out for cats, and traffic, and people like Mark Thomas. He needs to be somewhere safe, somewhere with other birds and plenty of food and shelter.'

Sean wasn't convinced, but agreed to visit the place Frank suggested.

'Only for a look,' warned Sean. 'If he doesn't like it...'

On Saturday morning they took Jeremy for a ride in Frank's car, out of the city, out into the country. Jeremy chirruped and Sean fed him. Bumping down a leafy lane, they turned into a set of gates and pulled up in a small car park. Frank led along a track beneath the dense canopy of trees until they came to a lake. Knots of people were sitting on its bank, fishing. There were no sounds of cars, or lorries or aeroplanes, only the occasional lapping of the water and the rustling of leaves, and the constant and wonderful cadences of birds singing.

Jeremy had grown silent, and was leaning his head at an angle.

'He's listening to the other birds,' Frank whispered.

Sean nodded.

'Put his nest on the ground and see what he does.'

Carefully, Sean laid the plastic nest on the grass and knelt beside it. Jeremy popped his head over the edge, looked round, and hopped out to start pecking at the leaf litter.

'Do you think he'll like it here?' Frank asked.

Sean nodded again, but he wouldn't look up, his eyes were

filling.

'We can visit him every weekend. I can show you how to fish and we can bring maggots to share with Jeremy.'

'But he won't know us, Grandad.'

'Yes, he will. While he's growing all his feathers we'll teach him a song, just like a mother bird would, and then we'll sit in the same place each time we come so he knows where to find us. It'll just be like you tapping on his nest.'

Sean reached out to tap on the plastic nest and immediately Jeremy hopped over for his maggot.

Sean smiled at him. 'He'll be safe here, won't he Grandad?'

Frank put his arm round his grandson and kissed the top of his head. 'Yes, he will, and he'll grow up big and strong and have lots of chicks all of his own.'

Thankfully he was. Sean insisted they visit the woodland every week. Sometimes Jeremy came for a maggot, sometimes he didn't, but Sean knew that he was safe and Frank was grateful for that.

Frank found his old binoculars and he and Sean learned to recognise other birds. He pointed out a heron, and once Sean saw a kingfisher dive into the water to catch a stickleback. Megan came with them occasionally, and she'd bring a proper picnic to set out on a cloth, not just sandwiches from a plastic box. Frank taught Sean how to fish while his mother read.

After Megan met Richard, he came along, too. Richard knew the names of trees, and the four of them would walk together along the nature trails. When Frank and Sean came on their own they'd leave the trails and hunt for tracks in the mud and the snow. Always Sean sang his tune and left food for Jeremy in their special place.

When the buds began to burst into leaf again, Sean stayed the night at his grandfather's house, setting his alarm especially early. Next morning, they needed a torch to find their way along the track to the lake. Even before the sky had started to lighten, the dawn chorus began, the birdsong rising all round them.

Sean turned round and round in wonder.

'It's so *loud*, Grandad.'

Frank hugged him close, knowing that Sean would remember this moment for ever.

They waited until the crescendo subsided before opening their sandwich boxes for breakfast. Sean sang his tune and scattered birdseed that he'd bought with his pocket money.

'Grandad, look. Is that Jeremy?'

At the edge of the undergrowth stood a lone male blackbird, proud and alert. They hadn't seen Jeremy for a few weeks, and in the deep shadows of the early morning it was difficult to recognise him. Slowly, Sean picked up the bait tin. He sang the tune again and reached out, a maggot in his fingers. The blackbird hopped across to take it from his hand and fluttered back towards the undergrowth.

'Jeremy! Grandad, it's Jeremy! But why isn't he eating it?'

From beneath the bushes, watchful and timid, a female blackbird hopped to Jeremy's side. He laid the maggot at her feet, and she ate it.

'Jeremy's got a special friend!' said Sean. 'They're going to build a nest!'

Jeremy hopped back and forth, feeding himself and his mate on the maggots Sean provided until Jeremy's mate grew confident enough to come for maggots herself.

They stayed a while and then the female flew off. Jeremy paused to cock his head and chirrup at them before following her. Sean leaned back in his grandfather's arms.

'He's got a special friend, just like Mummy. I wish I had a special friend,' he said.

Frank ruffled his hair. 'Can't I be your special friend?'

'You can't be a special friend,' Sean retorted. 'You're a special *Grandad!*' And he flung his arms round Frank's neck. 'The best Grandad *ever!*'

Commentary

Am I a grandparent, or a single working mother with a small child? All that belongs to the fiction. It was Jeremy – and we did call him that name – which triggered the story. He was found beneath one of our fir trees, in the naked state described, with no nest in sight. The kindest act, we decided, would be to put him out of his misery.

What can I say? For meat-eaters we are a sentimental bunch.

So began, more or less as described, Jeremy's care to fledgling. Alas, as Frank explains to Sean in the story *...you can't talk to him like a mother bird can. You can't tell him that he's got to watch for cats, and traffic, and people...* It was a car that dun it, m'lud – but I couldn't write that into the story for this particular market, hence the story's Disneyesque, lump-in-the-throat denouement.

To return to the story's inception, there was a small, featherless chick, and if it was to live it needed characters to care for it. Instead of looking for characters, I interrogated the chick: the *who*, *what*, *where*, *when*, *how*, and *why* of exploring possible story elements. The chick was homeless, parentless, cold, couldn't fend for itself, and was easy food for predators: by accident or design it had been discarded. Not a lot of laughs there. But it had given me a theme – abandonment.

Themes come in various shapes and sizes, and can be better understood if equated to fiction of yore where at the end could often be found the words *...and the moral of this tale is...* In modern fiction a theme is rarely stated, but its influence will thread through the story adding a subliminal weight. Keeping it simple and fairly direct helps it to glow through the text.

The chick had been abandoned. With one eye on the target readership of the chosen market, who could find themselves abandoned?

One-parent families immediately came to mind. A chick can equate to a child. A child without a father, left because his/her mother has to work so as to provide a home. Left to his/her own devices? Few stories from a child's viewpoint were taken by the chosen market, so that route was dismissed; when writing for a sale there is little point fighting odds stacked against the writer. The same reasoning made the father, rather than the mother, the abandoning parent.

The child needed to be left. With a child minder? With a family member? Working mothers tend to be highly organised, they have to be for their juggled roles to be successful, so I focused on the mother, made her tired and harassed, and dropped a problem into her ordered day: the childminder couldn't look after the child. Who would she turn to, at short notice, as a replacement? Her own mother? She's probably working, too. Make her older, retired? Too welcoming. What if there was no grandmother...? It was at this point in the thinking process that the story elements fell into place.

A person doesn't have to *be* abandoned to *feel* abandoned; a person doesn't have to suffer the death of a loved one to be locked in grief.

The mother stepped out of the story and I concentrated on the grandfather and the grandchild, who immediately transformed into a very young schoolchild and male. Grandfather and grandson has more symmetry than grandfather and granddaughter. The grandfather would be the viewpoint character, a man lost in his grief, unable to communicate effectively, unable to cope with the demands of a small child. This is fairly easy to convey as a viewpoint character, but how to convey similar emotions in a small child without making him seem sullen? It didn't take long to equip him with an electronic game, the noises it produces used as a distancing tool between the generations, and their repetition as an irritant to the grandfather and a flag to the reader. Once the two main characters were named, I could begin.

Because I wanted the story to be intimate between the generations, I didn't want to drip-feed back-story during its forward momentum. Readers needed to have a grasp of what had already passed, and the status quo of the characters, prior to the introduction of the abandoned chick. This is a tricky proposition, one I wouldn't normally recommend. Readers will not sit through a wodge of information before the action starts; editors will only read a few paragraphs before deciding to reject.

To give an intimation of action I chose to deliver the necessary information via speech, and what better way than via an argument. The mother character was called back into the story. Within the first few paragraphs it is seeded that Frank is passive, isn't taking care of himself properly, and that he's withdrawn from his usual pastimes, including fishing – seeded at this point to be picked up for the ending. I also made it seem that he's rather uncaring, allowing the reader to raise an eyebrow and wonder at the reason. Megan is portrayed as dominant, if somewhat shrill, Sean as lost within his own world oblivious to theirs, which readers soon realise is not the truth. Frank's perceived dilemma is stated overtly at the end of the first section, leaving his other problems unrecognised by himself but noted by readers who are likely to have experienced similar self-blindness in their own parents and grandparents; thus this also acts as an emotional hook.

The first line of the second section is part of the present: *Frank was awake with the dawn chorus* – seeding both the time of year and an image to be picked up for the ending – *fretting about the coming day* – emphasising his emotional state. However, the remainder of those two paragraphs are pure back-story that would never have worked if they'd been placed at the opening. Situated here, they offer a pause after the fast exchange of the argument and give depth to why Frank and Sean act the way they do.

Sean is described as *sidling by* rather than walking, *a pale and silent wraith in his drab school uniform.* I use those words, that tone, to create a mental image of a boy lost. At this point Frank doesn't notice, but later, when he watches his grandson leave for school, he does notice. This is the first step of his accepting that something is wrong, but at this juncture Frank is still too retreating to consider helping his grandson. He sees it in terms of a problem too large for him to cope with, too out of his league, and oscillates between anxiety attacks and being emotionally forlorn.

When Sean brings home the chick there is a moment of panic, this alerts the reader, followed by a description of the chick laid on Sean's palm, followed by a plaintive cry for help from Sean. Note how it is written: not merely described: Told, but enacted: Shown, so as to wring an emotional response from the reader.

There is a moment when Frank dithers, when he sees condemnation of all adults standing in the boy's eyes. This is the first major axis point, where what happens next depends on the main character's actions. Frank straightens his shoulders, and in that one movement readers know that he will straighten out his life, and will be supportive of Sean. Readers give a little cheer and read on to see how he manages it. In a story of this length there need to be small climaxes for readers to relate to emotionally, even if half the time they don't realise they are doing so.

As the story progresses so does Frank and Sean's relationship:
- Sean talks to a neighbour in search of food for Jeremy;
- Sean and Frank converse;
- Frank becomes a parent figure setting boundaries and explaining their reasons;
- Frank becomes the resourceful provider with the maggots;
- Frank and Sean provide a united front against Megan's reproach.

If viewed as a graph, a story's emotional plot-line should not rise from a flat line to a flat line. To keep readers engrossed the plot-line needs to look more like a series of 'W's of differing heights, the trend rising gradually towards the denouement. As problems arise the plot-line descends into a trough; as problems are overcome the plot-line rises to a peak, each time taking readers' emotions with it. The old adage that a writer plays God with the characters misses the point entirely. A writer uses the characters to play God with – to manipulate – readers' emotions.

When it has to be faced that Jeremy won't be safe in Frank and Sean's urban environment, Frank offers a Garden of Eden but, instead of dictating to Sean, places the onus on him to make the decision of where Jeremy should be set free. It becomes a meeting of minds for the greater good of Jeremy. They sit through a dawn chorus, connecting the end of the story to its beginning, and Frank and Sean go on to forge a lasting relationship sharing the grandfather-grandson outdoor pursuits of fishing and bird-watching.

Order has been drawn from chaos and all is right with the world, eliciting from the reader a smile and an emotional sigh. This is the ending I wrote, but it isn't the ending you've just read.

When I submitted the story it was accepted within days, with the proviso that <u>all</u> the ends be tied up neatly. Frank and Sean have found each other, so Megan must find someone, too, and Jeremy needed to be shown to have found a mate.

I baulked. There is a big difference between eliciting an emotional response from the reader and laying the emotional content on with a trowel so that a feel-good story turns into a risible fairytale. Besides, such an ending would dissipate the focus from Frank and Sean.

But an editor knows his readership and what is best for his magazine. A writer's intellectual integrity is not on an editor's horizon. Was I a prima donna or was I writing for the cheque?

You've read the ending.

Over To You

Write a story carrying an unstated theme. When finished you should be able to complete the sentence: This story is about..............

For possible starting points, mine proverbs – *all that glitters is not gold...a problem shared is a problem halved*. Lists of lesser known proverbs can be found on the internet.

Consider single words describing a state of being. These often end in -ment or -tion: embarrassment, enjoyment, addiction, dejection. If you are writing for a particular market, set these lists against its known readership, and its preferred gender and age range of lead character. Can a connection be made? A catalyst may be needed, as I had the chick.

Another way is to take a previously written story and interrogate it so that the sentence *This story is about*.............. can be completed. Try this on a short story published in a magazine, and then try it on one of your own. You may find that it is harder on your own. If so, list thematic possibilities, study each and chose one. Rewrite your story with this theme in mind, bringing it to bear in the setting, in the way characters interact, and in the manner the ending is brought to fruition. A light touch is advisable; don't ram the theme down your readers' throats.

The finished product should be a more focused piece of fiction which stays longer in readers' minds.

An Introduction To

A Bird In The Hand

Ideas for stories come from any number of sources, some less inspirational than others. *A Bird In The Hand* came from a hastily manufactured exercise during a lethargic meeting of the writers' support group I attend. No one had brought a work-in-progress for constructive criticism and, rather than call the meeting a loss, a sheet of paper was torn into pieces and members wrote a randomly chosen noun on each. Duly mixed, two were picked blind and handed to a third member charged to make an opening line. *I'll hold the <u>bag</u> and you get the <u>bird</u>* was only slightly modified by me for sense after my story was completed. Needless to say, members who took up the challenge each produced a spectacularly different story.

A Bird In The Hand

'When we get in there, I'll hold the bag and you get the bird.'

I nodded just the once, although I did not feel the decisiveness I hoped I was conveying.

The whole affair was foolhardy in my opinion, but the previous evening I had been left in no doubt that my opinion counted for very little. It had been too late to pull out, in fact there was no pulling out. It was the one thing I couldn't even contemplate. Whispers were many surrounding Johnson Sinclair. Almost certainly some were nurtured by the man himself to enhance his reputation, but who could tell what was fact and what was fiction where "concrete shoes" and "wheelchairs" were concerned. If my opinion counted for very little, it went without saying that my person was equally superfluous. Except, of course, that it seemed no one but me was able to identify a dead, probably frozen, immature acryllium vulturinum.

Driver wouldn't be able to, certainly. I doubted that he was capable of recognising a chicken in a supermarket's deep freeze cabinet. With his unblinking eyes and witless expression, he gave the impression of being a near illiterate.

Unlike Johnson Sinclair, whose curriculum vitae had been explained to me at length, if in loose detail, I knew nothing of Driver except that he was to be the wheelman. He never spoke, not even to Sinclair, the merest dip of his head answering in the affirmative to the two questions posed to him. He and Sinclair had had their own briefing prior to my arrival, that was obvious. I was an outsider, a *civilian* I believe is the term, to be tolerated for my specialist knowledge but to be trusted not at all. To add to his low IQ, Driver undoubtedly suffered a distinctive name and an even more distinctive accent. Such was their level of trust in me.

I didn't feel aggrieved, more amused at the childish subterfuge. It was such a far cry from the oily goodwill which had been poured on me by the management of the *Charleston* less than a month previously.

It is unfortunate, but the *Charleston* is now the only establishment in the area still admitting me to its tables. When my luck turned even there the manager turned likewise, from the ebullient *Call me Danny* to the po-faced *My name is Mr Marpollis*.

It wasn't that I was banned, simply not allowed to extend my credit. It became a game of cat and mouse between us. If Marpollis reached me before I'd passed through the foyer, I was ushered into an adjoining office and half my evening's entertainment subscribed to my account. Should I have won substantially, which wasn't often, the same detour was made upon leaving. I soon learned that if my wallet was handed over without complaint there would be no attempt at physical frisking. It seemed beyond their powers of wit that banknotes could be stashed in the top of a sock, or that chips could be slipped through a pocket into a purposely altered lining.

Even so, I was somewhat taken aback the evening Marpollis rushed across the foyer to welcome me like a long-lost cousin and reinstate my credit. He refused to discuss his change of heart except in that same, small, room.

'You have a benefactor,' he told me in reverential tones. 'Your account has been cleared.'

'The interest, too?'

'Especially the interest. Our tables are your tables.'

Even though my spirits were soaring, I had to acknowledge the nagging doubt.

'I don't know the identity of your benefactor,' Marpollis stated in answer to my question. 'The amount came by courier, in cash, in exchange for all documentation.'

Someone was holding my notes. Marpollis had sold me on to God-knows-who, no doubt for a substantial personal sweetener.

The urge to hit him between the eyes was immense, but I managed to resist the temptation. The cameras would only pick up the assault and the irksome Neanderthals he insisted on calling Security would be upon me before I could open the door.

And so my life had sailed quietly on, until three days ago when Johnson Sinclair had introduced himself. At first I mistook him for my benefactor.

'How naïve,' he'd said, and he'd chuckled.

It was when I began to make startled noises over his intended partnership plans that his true, odious, nature came to light. The choice was mine, he told me. But there was no choice at all, and the time scale was such that it was impossible for me to manoeuvre. The briefing was yesterday, the job tonight.

We left the car, and Driver, at the end of a line parked outside *The Wellington*. I had to admit that it had been good planning to mark the road and cone off the section as if one of the utilities was expected. The street lamp was out, too. Nothing was said about that, but I found it hardly a coincidence. The grimy Ford Mondeo was submerged in a pool of dark shadow, an undistinguished vehicle in a road full of cars, its bonnet pointing towards a triple junction for a choice of getaway route.

Oddly, it was not until Sinclair and I turned down the tenfoot between the Victorian terraces that my heart started pumping hard enough for me to hear the echo in my ears. I took deep, slow breaths to dilute the effect of the adrenaline pouring into my bloodstream, but it took time, and we were at the dog-leg between the high larch-lap fences before I felt totally in control.

Sinclair was ahead. I caught a momentary glimpse of his balding pate as it reflected the light from an uncurtained window above us. He had been adamant about what I should and should not wear, and how I should conduct myself, counting off each point on his fingers as if I were an imbecile: dark clothing, soft shoes, no coins to fall out of trouser pockets, and most definitely no wallet, credit cards or other means of identification. Was his uncovered head an oversight? More likely a vanity.

There was no moon, no street lamps, and lit rooms with uncurtained windows were certainly not the norm, but Sinclair drew up outside the rear of 71 Ashmount Gardens as if he had been measuring the distance. I ran into the back of him before I realised he had stopped. It was just a gentle touch, but he wheeled round on me like a rabid dog, grasping the front of my jacket.

'Stay here. Don't move from this spot.'

It had been arranged. It was in the carefully rehearsed script. I didn't need to be reminded like an amateur who forgot his lines. He let go of me and I took the opportunity to tug my jacket back into shape.

Shorter than me by a good four inches, with a body mass that could only be described as flabby, Sinclair had not struck me as an agile man. But his hands grasped the top of the fencing and I watched as his body followed, up and over and down the other side in a single fluid movement. At a given signal I had to follow. I was not sure that I could do it with such aplomb.

I waited, my gaze scanning the top rail for a vague shape darker than the enveloping shadows. The expected signal was not given. I worked my shoulders, flexing long dormant muscles ready for the assault on the fence. No signal came. A cool breeze drew fine strands of hair across my forehead, and to my ears brought the noise of an engine firing – a Ford.

My stomach churned. Logic told me that it couldn't be, that Driver would not have dared to leave his post, that not even at a run could Sinclair have made the distance— And then the Ford moved off, the engine's tone testifying that it was a Ford Focus.

I let out a sigh that seemed so loud I feared Sinclair might hear. I half expected to see his moon-like face peering at me over the barrier, but when I looked, there was nothing. I stood where I'd been instructed, aware of my shirt clinging coldly to my back, feeling foolish.

The noise of bolts being drawn made the hairs rise on my neck and fixed my attention on the fencing panel in front of me. Despite its seeming solidity in the darkness, and the wealth of weeds discernible at its foot, there was a gate. It opened perhaps six inches at its base, wider at the top, pouring forth a shaft of white light that could have graced any theatre's stage. It was so strong that Sinclair appeared in stark silhouette, his curled hand gesturing me forwards.

I stepped through the portal and stood squirming in the bright dazzle, aware that Sinclair was closing off our escape.

'The light!' I hissed. 'The light!'

He stepped to my shoulder, slipping his hands into the pockets of his jacket in a nonchalant manner. 'I disturbed a cat. The cat triggered the light. It'll go off in a minute. Don't waste the time; memorize the route to the door.'

He was so composed, so much in control. I felt inadequate, shaking in my shoes, expecting that at any moment a window would be thrown open and an accusing voice pierce the night. I glanced at over-looking bedroom windows, but all were in darkness save one, and that remained steadfastly mute.

An impenetrable black void enveloped us with a silence and a speed that was awesome. I could not see my own hands before me and had only a vague idea where the path lay. I had not done as instructed and would reap Sinclair's sneering contempt. Even now he would be standing by the house waiting for me to join him. I took a short step forward and found an arm barring my way.

'Wearing night glasses, are we? Let your eyes adjust.'

His eyes adjusted faster than mine, for I was just beginning to make out his figure when he moved ahead of me. I lumbered behind, trying to test my step before setting down my weight in case I kicked a bucket, or fell into an ornamental pond.

Searing light burned into my retinas and I stared up at its source, unable to move. Sinclair had increased his step to a determined lope. He was by the house wall in the shadow cast by the porch canopy before I marshalled my senses. I was already moving after him when he turned, but when he saw where I was the look on his face was unmistakable. In one furious movement he raised his arm, pointed a finger at me, and drove it towards the path beside him. Like an errant hound I dropped my head and went to heel.

I could feel his eyes boring into me, but could not summon the courage to meet his gaze. Instead, I stared down the garden, towards the shadowy fence and beyond, to the darkness where the safety of the tenfoot lay. He had not mentioned the security light. Not once during the detailed briefing had Johnson Sinclair mentioned the security light.

'They're there to deter amateurs,' he soothed. 'There are too many cats and too many trees. The get-up-and-check attitude soon palls after installation, and neighbours are notorious for not seeing, or hearing, a thing.'

The light winked out leaving a bright crescent after-image etched on my retina. At almost the same instant the quiet of the night was rent by the explosive shattering of glass at my shoulder.

'Nothing,' continued Sinclair, 'deters a professional.'

My heart felt as if it were lodged in my throat, and I could only pant my alarm. He had been so matter of fact during the briefing: *I'll take out the glass, open the window, reach through, and let you in the back door.* As my night-sight returned I realised that he was reaching through the shards of broken glass to open the window. He withdrew his arm and the frame swung towards me. I caught it out of instinct.

'The trick,' he murmured, 'is to make the noise only once. Its volume hardly matters.'

He half-turned his head to look at me, and a toothy grin lit his face with silent laughter. God only knew what emotion I was showing. The man was basking in my discomfort.

But it wasn't so much the noise that was making me quake now as the thought of the fingerprints he was leaving. I was not about to mention it, though, not again. We'd been through that one already, before the three of us had even reached the ramshackle Mondeo.

'And where do you think you're going on fine, warm evening, wearing leather gloves? Why not go the whole hog and buy yourself a pair of surgicals? Or even better, a red and black hooped sweatshirt and a bag with *Swag* written on the side.'

I hadn't let his sarcasm deter me, and pressed my case. Sinclair had exploded. 'That's the trouble with you educated know-alls. You know nothing. It's fire brigade policing out there. Scenes of Crime men rushing from job to job, smearing as many prints as they miss. It's a burglary we're about to commit, not murder. They won't even attend.'

He'd confiscated my gloves.

I put aside thoughts of fingerprints and watched as Sinclair backed against the wall to reach up inside the frame and find a purchase. With the same fluidity of movement he had used to scale the fence, he hoisted himself up, drew his legs under him, and disappeared into the dark maw of the unknown kitchen. A moment later there was the clicking of a lock. In less time than it would have taken me to enter my own residence, I was walking into a stranger's.

Gerald Talbot was a man as shadowy as Johnson Sinclair. I had first come across his name in learned ornithology papers while completing my Phd, and later in more commercial magazines writing articles about the sort of exotic birds seen rarely in captivity, or in the wild five degrees either side of the equator. His qualifications and publicised experience in foreign parts I had accepted without query. Only by chance did I later discover that most of his undoubtedly wide knowledge had been gained in the unlawful trading and transportation of exotic species. Now in his waning years, he was reduced to acting as taxidermist for those avaricious souls who could not bear to be parted from their dead, ill-gotten, possessions. Or, perhaps, what was secreted inside their dead, ill-gotten possessions.

Johnson Sinclair had not said, and I certainly wasn't going to be so bovine as to enquire, why it was that a man of his undeniably loutish talents had been secured for a measly petty theft, and I, in turn, coerced into accompanying him so that a dead bird could be correctly identified. Drugs? Diamonds? The ploy was too elaborate for something so mundane. A computer chip? But out of north-east Africa? The idea was as ludicrous as my predicament.

Sinclair produced a pencil-slim torch and flashed its beam quickly over the walls of the kitchen. The units were old and the melamine-faced doors hung on hinges too tired to support them. Food and dirty crockery had been left on the cluttered counters. The smell of rancid fat was nauseating, but there was not a sign of formaldehyde or feather.

Sinclair checked the refrigerator. I still couldn't believe that he would touch anything without the benefit of gloves. The man was too complacent, and he hadn't listened to a word I'd said. Acryllium vulturinum stand more than twenty inches tall in life. One would never have fitted in that refrigerator. Whichever room Talbot used in the pursuance of his craft, he did not use the kitchen.

The door to the hall stood ajar. The original leaded glass in the upper part of the front entrance allowed the weak street lamp beyond to cast grotesque shapes down the parquet. The light was enough to distinguish two adjoining doorways, and some sort of tall mirror-backed dresser which seemed to expand across the narrow walkway as if on guard. Halfway down the hall the spindled balustrade of the stairs began, reaching back and up to the first floor. Beneath it, to my immediate right, was an alcove used to store coats and all the paraphernalia of the house which had no other home.

Sinclair motioned for me to wait. He moved to the first of the closed doors, opening it tentatively to peer inside. He withdrew, closing the door again, and moved to the second. I wondered if there was a cellar, but could see no obvious entrance. We were going to have to mount the stairs. The thought made me shudder. Talbot wasn't home – Sinclair had been adamant about that during the briefing – but Sinclair had failed to mention the security light, hadn't he? Was there, for instance, a burglar alarm he'd overlooked?

I followed him up the staircase, careful to duplicate his every move. We made it to the first floor landing with only the single creak of a stair tread. From somewhere to our left there came the soft hum of an electrical appliance, a deep freezer by its tone. Sinclair led the way, criss-crossing the thin beam of his torch before him, leaving me in almost total darkness. At one point he stopped, and I had to do a little dance so as not to repeat running into the back of him.

I knew we'd found the place before Sinclair turned the door's handle. The smell of old fashioned taxidermy was unmistakable. Inside, the air was thick with it, as if Talbot had recently smashed a bottle of phenyl and had been lax in his neutralising. I could see the freezer, at least I could see its green light near the skirting, but I felt loath to cross the intervening floor space. Monochrome shapes were looming out of the shadows on every side. Talbot was an untidy man, and I feared that I might accidentally collide with something fragile.

'I need more light,' I whispered. 'I won't be able to distinguish anything in this.'

The white torch-beam flitted across the wall at my shoulder, and suddenly there was light, a full 150 watts of it, shining from a naked incandescent bulb suspended from the centre of the ceiling.

'What are you doing?' I gasped.

'Giving you light.' He walked ahead of me. 'You're educated. Think this is worth a bit?'

He'd picked up a bronze about a foot high and was twirling it in his hands, admiring it as if it were some trinket in a gift shop.

'For God's sake...'

Sinclair chuckled low in his throat. 'Amateurs. Always ready to piss their pants.'

He crossed the uncarpeted floor, standing the statue on top of the freezer cabinet while he pulled the curtains over the darkened window. Then he moved towards a battered filing cabinet and started to riffle through a drawer.

'Don't just stand there,' he snapped. 'You've a bird to find.'

I had an acryllium vulturinum to identify. I'd had no idea that I would be expected to plunder chest freezers to do so. I had thought that was, in part, what he was accompanying me for, but it didn't seem a good moment to argue demarcation lines.

His souvenir was a smooth-lined art deco piece, an angel with furled wings, or perhaps a nymph. I didn't look closely, but removed it from the lid and laid it on the bare floorboards out of my way. Talbot's business was not doing well, judging by the meagre contents of the freezer. There were two African eagles, a selection of native owls, and a dead dog – a King Charles' spaniel, by the look of it – all parcelled in reams of freezer wrap to avoid damage. Sinclair came to peer over my shoulder.

'It's not in here,' I told him.

He murmured something I didn't catch, moving away while I replaced the baskets as I'd found them. I closed the lid, listening to it seal with a slow wheeze, and turned in time to see the door to the room swing open. As my bowels transformed to liquid, Sinclair stepped to one side leaving me to face a bent old man with a walking stick.

'What are you doing here?' the cracked voice demanded.

Speech was beyond me. I didn't recognise Talbot from his magazine illustrations, but it could be no one else. And then he started advancing, and I realised that the stick he held was not to aid his balance. It was some short of slim, lethal-looking cudgel.

'Nice of you to join us, Mr Talbot.'

Both Talbot and I jumped at the sound of Sinclair's voice. As the door to the room swung back, my gaze became fixed on the slender bronze Sinclair was weighing in his hands. I retreated a step, and the chill from the freezer seemed to reach out and envelop me.

'Been naughty, haven't we?' Sinclair intoned. 'Done things we shouldn't, and not done things we should. Your benefactor is aggrieved.'

I gasped at those last words, gasped and held myself rigid. Movement seemed to phase into slow motion from that point. Johnson Sinclair raised the bronze and Talbot cowered back, but all three of us knew there was nowhere to run. I closed my eyes after the first sickening thud. Two more followed, and then there was silence. Talbot never cried out.

'It's over,' Sinclair said. 'You can open your eyes now, but I wouldn't suggest letting go of your stomach contents. The police might be a bit suspect where fingerprints are concerned, but I believe they're on the ball with their DNA profiling.'

Fingerprints. My fingerprints were everywhere: on the freezer, inside the freezer, on the wrappings of the birds...

I stared at Driver in the doorway. I couldn't comprehend that he was there and not waiting in the car. Mesmerized, I watched as Sinclair flicked his wrist to open a large polythene bag. The light caught the colourless opacity of his hand, and I realised that he was now wearing gloves. The hand which inserted the dripping bronze into the bag was encased in a surgical glove.

My legs began to buckle and I staggered, recoiling from the freezer behind me even as I put out a hand to save myself. My fingerprints were *everywhere.*

'A few deep breaths, that's all you need,' Sinclair advised. He held the bag up to the light, inspecting the bloodied contents. 'Just a precaution, you understand. Not that I think it's necessary. I'm sure witnessing Talbot's demise has been enough.'

He turned to nod at Driver, still standing sentinel in the doorway. 'Our friend is an educated man. He's not going to lose it.'

He raised a finger and pointed at me. 'Ah,' he said, 'I almost forgot. A deposit has been made on your behalf at a certain gaming establishment; a sort of goodwill gesture, and to cement the arrangement with your benefactor.'

'*Arrangement?* Who—'

Sinclair raised a fist at the same time Driver took a step forwards. I was quick to make submissive gestures.

'I have no idea,' Sinclair replied in the same even tone, 'but I'm sure you'll be contacted when your services are required. After all, that's the beauty of the arrangement, isn't it?'

Robbed of my anger I felt numb, cold, incapable of moving or thinking straight. This was simply horrific. Horrific.

'We're leaving now,' Sinclair said. 'Can we drop you somewhere? Be careful how you cross the floor, though. The Police tend to take a special interest in bloodied footprints.'

Commentary

Questions, questions, questions... that was what was asked of this opening line. It is the only thing that can be asked of any cold material that brings no inherent resonance. As I've repeated often in this book, the *who, what, where, when, how* and *why*. These are the keys that turn the lock, the codes that tilt the tumblers. *What if...?* is the pressure that opens the unlocked door. And like any good safe-cracker, a writer just has to persevere until it happens:

'I'll hold the bag and you get the bird.'

It wasn't given as speech but it became speech the moment it was written down. Who would say this to another? Someone in, or believes himself to be in, a supervisory role. What if the supervised resents being supervised? Ah, the glimmer of a problem; I fixed this possibility for later. No story can survive without a problem. If there is no problem the writing becomes a mere study.

Why does it need two people to get the bird in the bag? It hardly sounds as if it is a plastic toy, though it could, of course, be a poacher's dead pheasant. What if it is real and fighting? What if it is a protected species? This sounded promising so I followed a tangent considering ospreys and golden eagles and the stealing of eggs, but found it to be a moribund line of enquiry.

First choices often are. After all, if they come so readily to my mind they'll come readily to the minds of readers, and which readers want to spend time on a story where they are ahead of the action, not chasing to catch up? I let this tangent drift into oblivion and would suggest this course to any writer wrestling with a storyline. First thoughts are warm-up thoughts, and nearly always lead to better things.

What if the bird was real but not fighting? What if it was dead? Who would want a dead bird, want it enough to take someone along to help get it in a bag? How big is this bird? No, not *help* to get it, but *to get it*. Always read what's there and not what you think is there. The supervising character is *instructing* the subordinate character to get the bird – why? Because no one can recognise the bird except the subordinate – why? Because he's an expert on birds. The resentful expert is there in a subordinate capacity being supervised because... because he is there under duress. Voila! Flags were waving, bells were ringing. More important, my imagination had lit.

Who is the supervisor and what is he holding against the expert to make him compliant? I had no idea. I needed to know more about the expert: his early life, his current life, his foibles, his failings. The clue would be hidden in his background.

Character-building, even for a short story, can be a long, drawn out affair, especially on paper. It certainly isn't an amalgam of random choices. The pieces need to fit with the precision of a 3D mosaic. Suffice to say my expert had a doctorate in the mating rituals of specific exotic bird species, was expected to gain this qualification by his peers and his parents, who had enough money to fund him through his extended education and the world travelling required. All this had fed a cutting arrogance and sense of superiority which had grown worse as his disenchantment with his life increased. His foible, his fix, that his academic standing could not plug, was gambling, gambling at the tables of a casino. His problem was that he wasn't good at it, in fact was seriously bad at it, therefore leaving himself vulnerable to...? Organised crime. I had my supervisor: some sort of underworld enforcer.

From here it was a short jump to realise that the bird was not being sought for itself, but for either what it held (too clichéd for the storyline but ideal for the expert to believe) or what it signified, therefore a parakeet was neither going to be big enough nor exotic enough. A surf of the internet produced more than enough exotic birds to choose from, and I decided that an acryllium vulturinum had a sufficiently complicated and exotic name, and was of sufficient size, to hold possibilities. Making it an immature specimen, and therefore of different coloured plumage from an adult, would help bring the expert to centre stage even more. I had my two leading characters.

So... the supervisor takes along the expert to recover the bird, but who is holding the bird? The most logical person to be holding a dead acryllium vulturinum would be another expert. A first choice? Certainly, but a considered first choice. Bear in mind that I am writing a short story and have a finite number of words to play with. If I'd been writing the subplot of a novel the decision would doubtless have been different.

Some stories are a hard slog right through to the very end. Other stories have a moment of epiphany when all the pieces fall into place. This one did, right here, in the form of "The old king is dead. Long live the new king". The criminal underworld does not drag someone, even an expert, off the street to aid a project, not without the wherewithal to ensure that person's silence, and it certainly wouldn't go to all that trouble without an ulterior motive. Motive comes from characters.

With the background to the characters and the plot route roughed out, a decision was needed on the protagonist, the character through whose eyes and mind the story would be conveyed. When in doubt go for the person with the biggest problem – in this story it is the supervised expert.

First person viewpoint or third person viewpoint? I knew the supervisor and the expert were on a quest to find a bird, and that my protagonist was going to be the resentful expert there under duress. In such a predicament he was not likely to be doing a lot of speaking, but he was liable to be doing a good amount of internal grumbling. To put this across to readers successfully, first person viewpoint would be the easiest vehicle. The tone of delivery, and the syntax used in the make-up of the sentences, would come from his background meshed with how he felt at the time. So, mindful of arrogance, resentment, money and level of education, I knew how he would sound and how he would hold himself.

Note, however, that there is no mention of his age nor any description of him within the story. Characters, certainly main characters, should be built from the inside out. His age and what he looks like hardly matter, as a re-reading of the story will testify. In keeping, there is also little physical description of either Driver or Johnson Sinclair. If the protagonist believes himself culturally and intellectually their superiors, why would he consider them in depth? They are described only in relation to how the protagonist regards them.

Johnson Sinclair was given that name to clothe him in an aura beyond the norm. John Sinclair would not have worked nearly as well in marking his role. Gerald Talbot, on the other hand, was given an old fashioned name and a drum roll via the protagonist's memories, which drops to a pervasive sneer when less savoury aspects of the man's life are recalled. It is enough to give readers an idea of Talbot's bearing so that when he is encountered in the flesh the protagonist cannot recognise him from his earlier photographs, such has been his fall from grace. This also, by the end of the story, acts as a mirror for what is likely to befall the protagonist.

As humans, we believe we have free will and are, to a great extent, in control of our own lives. When that free will is curtailed the tendency is for us to take small victories where we can: the secretary who purposefully brews bad coffee for a colleague making life difficult; the disgruntled employee who "fines" the employer a day's "sickie".

Our conceit is that we neither see nor look for the bigger picture, and neither does the protagonist, the unnamed expert. Instead, he takes pleasure in foiling his adversary's discovery of gambling chips and banknotes. He is contemptuous of those who have financial and physical control over him, believing himself of a superior intellect and therefore above such inconveniences. But read between the lines to realise that he is contemptuous of the world at large, and is, in fact, a solitary and sad figure who has cut himself off from humanity. If this scenario had happened to you, how many people could you turn to for advice and aid? The expert has painted himself into a corner by his attitude towards his fellow man and therefore is easy prey because he is a man alone. This became the theme, which gradually rose to hover above the gathering story elements: the fallacy of perceived control.

Finally should be considered the reader's required reaction. Have you considered your own reaction? You've been in the company of a man who is threatened, has witnessed a murder, a man knowing that he's caught in a trap, probably for life. How do you feel about that, about him? Did you smile?

Do you feel the way you do because the protagonist is unnamed and not described, or is it because he is an unsympathetic character? Would he have become a more sympathetic character had he been named and described? Would you have felt differently at the end of the story?

A reader can empathise or sympathise or view with detached interest. Ensure you know which you wish to elicit in your reader before you start writing.

Over To You

Don't listen to people who insist that to work, fiction must come via the divine hand of inspiration. Like as not they've never written anything longer than a shopping list. Fiction, like most arts and crafts, is honed through sheer hard work. Inspiration, like talent, can be nurtured. Neither will happen unless you make them happen by practising.

Learning to cut a path through the jungle of possibilities that lay between idea and first line is equally valid. Ideas rarely come in neat, usable parcels. Question, question, question, that is the name of the game, so question some of these first lines:

- Mrs Jeffries' house is a receptacle for the bizarre
- I knew what I'd done as soon as the door closed
- It wasn't that bad, not really
- The wall felt sticky beneath his palm
- 'So, do you want to come?'

Each part line – except for the last, did you note the lack of full-stops? – holds clues to its inherent viewpoint, tone and tension. Don't merely read the words, absorb the meaning held prisoner in the phrasing. Adding meaning to phrasing in your own fiction lifts a story above the norm. That's why every word counts.

An Introduction To

Harvester World TZ29-4

Sometimes ideas root and seem to produce sturdy shoots, but the completed story refuses to reach for the light. It becomes a work-in-progress stretching across months or even years. While other projects come to rapid fruition, only a sporadic fluttering of a half-curled leaf shows that this story still holds life. It won't die, yet it won't live, and its continued presence irritates.

This was one of those stories, and it proves the theory that no partly completed writing should be binned. There is a time for every idea.

Triggered by two television documentaries watched many months apart, it went through three from-scratch rewrites before I hit on this method of conveyance. It was always going to be of the SF genre, that was never in doubt, but I'm a short story writer who works close in to her subject, when on this occasion what was needed was to combine that proximity to the bigger picture. Not only did I need to step back, I needed to borrow skills from novel-writing.

Harvester World TZ29-4

My arm is broken, I know it is. My fingers won't respond, and there's no denying the jagged lump pushing up through my skin. The painkillers should kick in any time, but this is it. Read it as it is and breathe the air. This is the end.

Odd that I should think of Mercel now. It had been his saying back on the belt. We didn't want to listen then. We should have done.

Rumours had been rife since someone in Coms had illicitly passed on the decode. *Shut-down imminent. Total relocation.*

The difference the knowledge made to my co-workers was undeniable. There seemed to be smiles beneath the transparent masks, eyes twinkling under the brow-lights. And people spoke, too, not only of the future, but of other, more trivial, matters.

Not all communication was optimistic, though; it never is. There were counter-rumours. On our shift the loudest voice was Mercel's.

'Not us,' he kept saying, 'not the Drones. Coms – yes. Trans – yes. Meds – sure. But us? Read it as it is and breathe the air.'

Usually he was ignored, but I was in the rec chamber when he finally goaded a response from Salul.

'Were we hallucinating? Didn't you test with the rest of us? Wasn't your status redesignated?'

'Sure I tested,' he said. 'Everyone tested. It's all a blind.'

'Relocation is well overdue. We've only been kept here to ensure the franchise doesn't lapse. The belt is mined out. The sections we're taking aren't worth their transport.'

'And you think Genetics are?'

It was the one possibility no one put voice to. We watched as Mercel took an oxy-tab from his arm pack and fed it into his life-support. The rec chamber was quiet enough for us to hear the slow fizz as it engaged. He seemed to look at us individually as he adjusted the pressure setting on his face mask, an automatic movement we all made countless times a shift.

'Read it as it is,' he said, 'and breathe the air.'

He hadn't been right, of course. But he hadn't been wrong, either. We should have questioned more, shouldn't have gone along so willingly. But maybe that was part of our gene make-up, something that had been bred into us. Who can tell? What does it matter now? It's over.

The bulletin was posted not long after. Some of the language wasn't what we were used to, but the message was clear enough. There had been a pass rate on the skills audit, and in accordance with the Contract a relocation team would be arriving with a resource pack. The immediate implementation of Security-7 was not unexpected, but for those due their end-of-tour off-world Rec it was a blow to have the facility withdrawn. Mercel, especially, saw it as a logical progression.

'Entrapment. Disassociation. Termination.'

The reloc team arrived sooner than anyone had dared hope. It seemed to take even Coms by surprise, but we put that down to the Security-7. We'd expected the processing to be kept to downtime, but we were called in-shift. The presentation wasn't a remote, either, but an inter-personnel. The co-ordinator wore the standard grey over-suit and was rigged in all the equipment we carried, but without the ingrained ore dust he looked ludicrous. We should have suspected then.

There were charts to show us where the relocation site was in relation to the belt and the off-world rec-stations we used, but few were interested. We wanted to know about the site itself. What would we be mining? Could the targets be met any easier than on the belt?

'Conditions?' With an exaggerated smile the co-ordinator

unbuckled his life support and let it fall at his feet. 'The atmosphere is breathable!' His brow-light followed the mask. 'All work sites and accommodation blocks are situated *top-side*. Shifts will be for the duration of natural light only. You will be harvesting organic vegetable product.'

What did we know about organic vegetable product? We were drone miners, doing the work machines couldn't. We had never seen even the inside of the orbiting hydroponics unit.

They talked fast then, the relocation team. Famine, kept hidden under a Security-6, was devastating the old worlds. Reformist had supplanted Expansionist theory. A second generation Contract had been sealed. Basic sustenance was the priority, and TZ29-4 had been identified as a possible harvester world. The belt carried the closest non-reserved workforce. The skills audit had proved positive. All that was needed was our commitment.

They did well nurturing our commitment. The experience chamber was beyond expectation, beyond anything the rec-stations offered. Soft breezes, natural starlight, textured growing medium beneath our feet, verdant foliage so bright a colour it hurt the eye... Some couldn't take the intense scents and were ill where they stood. I hung on to my stomach contents, but only by keeping my life-support primed and my face mask close. During the de-brief worries were voiced about the poisons in the atmosphere, but we were assured that this was natural, no worse than any hydroponics unit. Rooted life-forms released gases just as Genetics did. They, too, were living organisms.

'Capable of communication?' Mercel again, adamantly hostile.

'Among itself, perhaps, for reproductive purposes, but sub Level 1.'

'So even if it's aware it's being culled there will be no chance of it demanding a Contract.'

Everyone looked at Mercel. Even I felt the frisson. It was history, though some said folklore, why the original Contract for Genetics had been forged.

'Organic vegetation was the founding code of Planet Earth, the First Planet. Without it no biped life would have been possible. Our ancestors, the ancestors of us *all*...'

We could have been listening to a compulsory data-disc during a Four-Tour Rehab. Ecological control was mismanaged... aberrations within the populace led to famine...the organic vegetation recovered but had lost its potency...there was more famine, more aberration...

I think it was the co-ordinator's sudden silence which caught our attention. When he continued his tone was less assertive.

'It's happening again,' he said. 'One by one the harvester worlds are losing their potency. TZ29-4 has been identified as a possible replenishment source, but speed is a Priority-9. The facility has to be running at 30% capacity by the onset of the Magnian Curve or the first shipments—'

He carried on speaking but his voice was lost in the uproar. I saw Mercel gesticulating, too, but I never learnt what he was saying.

When the furore had calmed the bounties were outlined. If the vegetation was as viable a food product as first indications showed, TZ29-4 would be liable for up-grading to residential standing. Eligible females could, if they wanted, have their Worker status redesignated. Progeny could be produced.

'Not bio-genetic host-pools,' the co-ordinator emphasised, 'individual Motherhood.'

Individual Motherhood. For Genetics. It was unthinkable. The cut off would be 2-5. Not one female on the belt carried more than a 2-4. We would all be eligible. The relocation team understood Commitment. It was we Genetics who were blind.

What noise is that? A rustling? A dripping? I don't know which I fear more: the vegetation or Security. This unifab is shielded; I should be safe. There again, TZ29-4 is supposed to be a second Earth. It's not.

Trans was functioning at full capacity ferrying equipment and personnel from the belt to the long-haul ship the reloc team had brought. The experience chamber had been refitted aboard, and while the jump was made we were put through a stabilization programme to lessen the effects of the atmosphere change. The reloc team wanted us to hand in our life-supports, but we held on to them.

It was a good decision, the only good decision we made, because the experience chamber was nothing compared to standing on the terrain of TZ29-4. We all threw up. Some couldn't stand. There had been no mention of the gravity difference, no mention of the vapour-filled atmosphere. A company of Con-Drones had been shipped in before us to begin work on the facility. I don't think any of us would have survived if we'd had to start from virgin terra.

We could probably have coped with the vomiting and diarrhoea, but sleep deprivation rose to critical. Working on the belt, the low vibration of drilling machinery was the most that had intruded on our down-time allocations. I'd encountered rain in the experience chambers the rec-stations leased, most of us had, but these were rainstorms so torrential that roofs had given way on the first drop unifabs. The remainder had been strengthened before our arrival, but not proofed against sound. Even communication within the same unifab space was beyond us. Then, without warning, four or five lighttimes after landfall, we were equalised, and sleep came to us all despite the darktime rainstorms.

'So what are we being given?' Mercel wanted to know. 'We can't be supplied through the life-support any more; we're not using them. It must be through the food.'

The rest of us were just grateful to be equalised.

Induction started the same lighttime despite the cumulative effects of fatigue; looking back it was probably because of them. We swapped our grey suits for red, and took a tour of the facility. The Con-Drones wore white. They weren't communicative, but we all knew what a priority bounty system entailed so none of us questioned their attitude. What we did question was the electrified processing area and the elevated packing house.

'The fence is a visual reminder that you are entering the area. It isn't charged, only the ground it encloses.'

Non-conductive grilles lay over bare soil, the only bare soil we'd seen so far. There was a low sizzling as we walked, a dragging of static on our legs.

'The net is sunk far enough beneath the surface to prove no hazard. The grilles are more for ease of movement after the rains than as a protection from the net. The vegetation thrives on the culling process. The net deters regermination in an area needed permanently clear.'

'What's the charge?'

'It's still experimental. Down to a 6-5, I think.'

We moved on towards the elevated processing block. Mercel stood alone assessing the generator housing. Without warning he lifted his leg and dug the heel of his boot through a grille connection. There could have been sparks, I'm not sure, the starlight was so bright, but there was a definite crackle and the acrid smell of burning.

'Malfunction?' I asked.

'Higher charge,' he said.

The first phase processing was on-line, but at less than 1% of the envisaged target it was a simple run-through to test efficiency. Culled, the organic vegetation looked like lengths of fibrous conveyor strip discoloured to a variegated green. It was explained that it was the sap that carried the highest proportion of nutrients, which was why a cauterization blade was used in the culling.

In situ the vegetation looked nothing like conveyor strip. It stood in thick clumps rising from a knotty bole, each leaf no wider than my hand, each bole packed so close to the next as to prevent passage between. Individual leaves stood erect a head taller than anyone in our party, and had a sheen to their surface that I had not noticed in the processing plant. They moved, too, stirred by the breeze, creating an odd rustling effect to our ears.

There were some who later said they were communicating, but even now I don't accept that. There was no need for external communication. They were connected below ground, just like the net.

We were split into parties according to our skills designation and the programme began the next lighttime. Free of life-support and cramped conditions, our work rate soon reached peak efficiency. The first load lifted off-world well before target, and the white-suited Con-Drones went with them. We were on our own. Just before the Magnian Curve disabled Trans and Coms alike, a message was received.

Potency tests +5. Full production schedule.
Target attainment will ensure upgrading.

Residency status was within our grasp; Motherhood was within mine. It drove us on. Associations became more complex, more intense. It was a Mother's prerogative to choose the male to father her progeny. A man already aligned to a possible Mother stood more chance of being chosen. I'd never known such attention. The only one I wanted was Mercel, but he showed no interest, not to me, not to any of the Mothers.

'I don't want to be considered,' he told me.

We had an argument about it.

'It isn't that I'm incapable of the emotional bond,' he said. 'I don't want you to be a host. I don't want any of you to be a host. It's too soon. The Authority never moves this fast, not with anything, especially upgrading.'

I accused him of seeing conspiracy everywhere.

'That's because it's there,' he said. 'Read it as it is and breathe the air.'

I didn't listen. None of us listened. TZ29-4 was going to be New Earth.

*

I can't stay here. I've got to make a run for Net-6 before the rains start. Romak doesn't need me. I'm an aberration to him. What if I'm an aberration to Security? Maybe they won't let me enter Net-6.

Those of us who worked in the processing house had no true impression of the vegetation's reproduction capability, but transferred to the culling gangs we soon learned.

Culling finished well before darktime so that the harvested vegetation and the gangs could be back within the net and undercover before the rains started. The following lighttime the field of cull would be waving with fronds as high as our knees.

It grew almost before our eyes, or rather, our backs, for the immediate culling line did not regenerate, except where a track was cut at 90 degrees to the line to create a second culling front. It could be guaranteed that by the tenth metre cut into the swathe, the first would be re-shooting. That was why I was transferred, to make up a secondary dampening unit behind the main culling gang.

Despite the cauterization blades, the gases the shoots emitted were noxious, and the life-supports we'd used on the belt came into their own. The problem was that stocks of oxy-tabs were low. We were going to have to find some other way of dealing with the shoots.

That was how the Meds became involved. They came to take samples for testing. The first visit they wore the regular red workgear. The second they were equipped in full protection suits, complete with life-support. We asked why. There'd been an accident in the labs, they said; a precaution, they said. We asked what sort of an accident, but the Meds were evasive.

'If it can happen in Med it can happen in the field,' insisted Mercel.

It took some time but he persuaded the gangs to stay within the net until we received answers. With capacity halted the Meds had no choice. A non-cauterizing blade had been applied and the sap had made contact with skin causing an allergic reaction. The Med-Tech was now on enforced downtime and, as the unit was small and all personnel were specialists, for the good of the facility it had been decided to take extra precautions until the tests had been processed.

With the end of the Magnian Curve in sight and the targets not fulfilled, the gangs agreed to resume. Mercel tried to talk them out of it, but without the targets residency status wouldn't be conferred. I think his stridency marked him then. In fact, I'm sure it did.

We made the targets. Residency was accorded and with it Worker redesignation, but for me not Mother-1. I was designated Mother-3. The increase in population had to be gradual. I had to wait my turn. The disappointment was minimal. I was a Mother, a status I would never have achieved on the belt.

A gynaecological unit was shipped in to us. There was a fervour among the Drones, among the Mothers. We worked as close as was possible to the onset of the darktime rainstorms. We would carve ourselves a New Earth from TZ29-4.

Salul was the first to be diagnosed as bearing. She died halfway through her term. If the Meds knew then what was happening, no one outside the unit was told.

All Mother-1s were taken into Med for observation. Two foetuses died inside their hosts. One was aborted due to deformities. The rest were delivered before full term because they were so well developed. The losses were attributed to the inherent dangers of individual Motherhood. If host-pools were despised, at least we understood why they had been introduced.

There was a meeting and the leading Gynaeco laid it on the line for us. They had been unable to find a cause for the initial problems, and as such couldn't ensure they wouldn't arise again. We were offered the option of donating to a host-pool. Nobody took it, and Mother-2s were allowed to conceive.

I could hardly make my way through my habitation block for

potential fathers. From being flattered by the attention I was beginning to be unnerved.

Mother-2s were taken into the unit, but Mother-1s were not released. An extension was erected. More equipment arrived from off-world, more Med personnel. Visiting was curtailed. Deliveries of the Mother-2s were not announced. Rumours began to circulate, not just of the condition of the Mothers, but of natural conditions of the first Earth. Word was that vegetation and humans had not been the only life-forms. There had been secondaries – quadrupeds and air-bipeds – which had lived among the vegetation as the humans had. Why were there no secondary life-forms on TZ29-4? Why was there only vegetation? We didn't know it then, but all Coms personnel were replaced.

Mother-3s were denied conception facilities, temporarily, we were told. I was devastated. What status was a Mother if not allowed progeny? Two asked for off-world trans. It was refused. We had been quarantined.

It was then that part of Net-1 failed. The control boards remained positive, which accounted for the delay, and nothing had been heard because of the rain. The wreckage was evident in the lighttime. So was the strength of the vegetation. It had broken through the net and bored through the base of Accommodation-3. More ominous was its size. During a single darktime in the culling field it grew knee-high. Round Acc-3 most of it stood full height.

We cut through to the block fast enough, but it took nearly half the lighttime to dampen the shoots and charge a secondary net. I was grateful not to draw for the evac team. Everyone accepted that there were going to be no survivors in the twisted remains of Acc-3, and I didn't want to be the one to have to load Mercel's body in its sack.

The evac team found more than bodies and vegetation. They found optics. We broke through the walls of the other Acc-blocks, of the elevated processing house, the packing store.

Optics were everywhere. We had been recorded from the moment we landed. Mercel's death had been recorded. We weren't quarantined; we'd been transported from the belt to a long-term lab facility. The Contract for Genetics means nothing. We are here to be modified.

Am I being recorded as I huddle here? I must assume so. I must assume that my being here has been accepted as part of the data collection. That's why I could gain a cauterization blade with such ease. That's why there's been no rescue attempt.

I must rescue myself. I have to make it to Net-6 before darktime. The dripping has stopped. The rustling, too. My legs are good. *Move!*

We moved as a body when the optics were discovered. We moved to the Med centre and demanded entry to the Mothers. We had expected dependent progeny. They were half-grown adults, tall and gangling, with nervous, flitting eyes. And they all looked alike: dark hair and tinged skin with a sheen I recognised from the culling fields. All reached for the protection they felt only their Mothers could give. With strained, grim faces, their Mothers hugged them close. A bond of mixed emotion went out to them. It could have been me. For a reason I could not explain, I wanted it to be me.

The off-world Security team moved with speed and determination. No one had heard a transport. No one knew they were waiting. Resistance was crushed and those remaining were driven into the Acc-blocks. It was while tending the wounded that we realised we were all contaminated. Blood which should have been a dark red was a pale pink.

What colour is yours, Romak? The pigment in your skin has a green tinge that reacts to the starlight. They think I don't notice, but I do. Your violence goes in cycles, too. They call it Frustration Complex – a body too mature for the mind that controls it – but it's not. It's a surge heralding a change. What change has there been this time, Romak? What will I see when I go out this door?

I spent so long hooked to those monitors; not a Mother, but an individual host. I think I see Mercel in you sometimes, in the way you tilt your head, little gestures you make with your hands, but that's not who – what – was contained in the fertilization pod.

There have been other facilities, haven't there, on TZ29-4. Is ours third generation? Fourth? They won't say, but I think you know. In the culling field, your bare feet firmly in the glutinous soil, you used to stand for an entire shift just staring into the wall of green. Was it communicating with you, Romak? Or were you communicating with those who'd gone before you? How many generations does it take to forge a new Genetic? No data-disc I ever saw held that information.

Darktime is coming. The rains will start soon. I may have left it too late to get back to Net-6. Perhaps that's my intention.

My arm doesn't hurt now. There's no feeling at all below the shoulder, just a dead weight that I need to clutch. The hand is cold, very cold. I wonder if they'll amputate. I don't want them to experiment any more. I'd rather they terminate.

There's a popping sound. I know what it is. The shoots are growing, attacking the unifab, trying to reach me. I have to get out.

The connecting door's pressure pad still works and the plate glides aside. The stench! I try to cover my nose, but already my eyes are beginning to flood. The area is green with boot-high leaf. Beyond the broken net the vegetation stands, a sentient, rustling mass.

'Romak?'

I expected him to be here. I've caught him before, lying in the culling field, oblivious to the gases, letting the shoots whisper round him. I expected him to be here. He's not.

Spots of rain splatter the shoots in front of me. It is still light enough to see, yet the rains come. I make a run for the causeway, a run for Net-6.

It's blocked. I can't believe it. The vegetation stands full height, a barrier across the causeway. The rain begins to pound against me, making the vegetation sway. Romak!

Others step from the vegetation with him, other progeny I've never seen. Tall, hunger-lean, they've divested themselves of their clothing and their bones show through darkened flesh, variegated and with a sheen seen on the leaf fronds, a sheen to take the cascading water of the darktime. Romak is holding something. The light is fading fast now; I can't tell what it is. The ground is liquefying beneath my boots, the huge raindrops pummelling me down. I slip, catch myself, slip again. The shoots are reaching for my knee. I fall among them, lie among them, their gases making me retch, their fronds rustling over me.

I hear the sizzling, catch the pink-hued light in my peripheral vision. I didn't think it would work in the rain, but it does. Romak is holding the cauterization blade, and he knows how to operate it.

There's nothing of Mercel in his bearing now, everything of the impassive Med-Techs. Read it as it is and breathe the air. This is not to be the end for me. I wish it was. I truly wish it was.

Commentary

The spark for this story came from watching two television documentaries.

One was on Progeria, the rare but devastating condition in children which causes rapid aging due to an accidental genetic mutation. While I was still sympathising with mothers whose children were stricken, the writer in me was thinking: *what if* the genetic mutation wasn't accidental but introduced; *what if* the mother, the entire society, was unaware; *what if* it wasn't the first time this had happened?

I was reminded, too, of another documentary I'd seen, on the possibility of growing organs for transplant patients rather than harvesting organs from donors. The team had successfully grown human ear tissue on the back of a laboratory mouse. Lab mice today, tomorrow...? And how much easier would it be if it was out-of-sight, out-of-mind? From these two documentaries came the premise for the fiction.

The genre self-selected, as did a dystopian world – but which world? Ours? I couldn't see how that could be handled successfully. Too much recent history would seep in, if not through my keyboard then through readers drawing on their own experiences.

In its first and second incarnations, I concentrated on the mother and child aspect, shadowing in back-story only faintly and describing the planet and the reason for being there hardly at all. I chose different protagonists, used first person and then third person viewpoints, but there wasn't the necessary depth to the fiction. Characters were speaking and moving in what amounted to a vacuum. It took a while for me to realise that the fiction lacked enough anchorage points for readers to connect emotionally to the mother's plight.

When readers pick up any work of fiction they are making a conscious decision to let slip their own, everyday reality, and to immerse themselves in an alternative, virtual reality. This they subconsciously build from anchorage points in the opening text, flashes of solid information into which readers can safely tie their imaginations as they enter the fiction: *time*, *place*, *focus character* and an *intimation of the problem*. After that, given enough clues, readers' imaginations can build the fictional reality as the storyline develops.

I had a woman – for ease I decided to stick with the norm of a woman – who had been duped into becoming pregnant, but it was all going terribly wrong, shattering her projection of nurturing life. This gave me only two out of the four anchorage points. No wonder the story was not writing well. Back to asking the usual questions.

Where was she? *Who* was she? *What* was she? *How* was she? *Why* was she? *When* was she?

I was certain that she was in the future, the far future; it made the story easier to write and I didn't have to look too critically at my own society which considers it acceptable to use lesser mammals as, well... guinea pigs; the term says it all. And at a stroke I had the setting to my story: a controlled environment that the guinea pig – the woman – didn't recognise as a laboratory. I needed to find another world, and with it an enclosed society.

People in our world work within closed societies all the time: oil workers on rigs out in the ocean, builders of highways through desert or jungle. I needed to project something similar into our future, into space. *What* were they doing there? *Why* was it an enclosed society? *How* did they live? Back to the usual questions.

Slowly an impression of them coalesced: what they were doing, the background to their society, how they were the same as us yet different. With these people shimmering within reach I went through a similar process to discover why they would move – by coercion or enticement? – and what they would move to.

On Earth, almost throughout history, resources have been sought and fought over. For us it is fuel, food and transformable minerals that can be bartered for either. Why would it be different in the future? By polarising these I could produce two very different environments: one the society was immersed in, one it would move to. These became my mining belt, where the people would live below the surface and need life-support to survive, and a planet of dense vegetation capable of providing sustenance where the people would live on the surface and not need life-support. I considered this. How would I feel if the move was about to happen to me? Moving from the one to the other must seem like the fulfilling of a dream. Or a myth. What if these people mistakenly thought of it as Eden because they had only the vaguest notion of what Eden, what Earth, had been like?

Throughout the slow forming of these connections, the next from the previous, the two worlds began to take on colour and mass, and with it the enclosed society. The stumbling point was the vegetation to be harvested. To make it more obvious to readers that something was amiss, the vegetation could not be as diverse as we know on Earth. Could it be a mono-culture, a single plant form?

Across from my favourite chair at the time stood a pot-bound houseplant, Sansevieria trifasciata: known as Mother-in-Law's Tongue or Snake Plant. Its rhizomes were crowded, its variegated yet oddly striped leathery leaves stood erect and defiant. Every part of this plant is poisonous if ingested; merely handling it can cause a skin irritation. *What if* it grew three metres tall; *what if* it stood so crowded in open habitat that a human could make no path between its sharp-edged leaves; *what if* the climate was perfect for a fast regrowth; what if it communicated via its root system? I had my vegetation to be harvested.

How could I put all this, and more, across to readers via a short story? There was so much of the setting, and the back-story, that needed to be hinted at, if not exactly explained. The story's timescale was also extended. In truth I was attempting to compress a novel, or at least a novella, into the length of short fiction. My proposed market took no more than 5,000 words, and the story would have a better chance of acceptance if considerably shorter. Although some authors write to the natural length of the story and cut, I feel that this only works well if the natural length is close to the required length. If more than 10-15% is cut the structural balance can be severely compromised.

I borrowed a technique from novel-writing: twin storylines evolving in parallel. One would concentrate on the immediate, the other on the back-story. The present tense would be used for one and the past tense for the other so as to accentuate the difference, but both would be conveyed by the same character, in first person, to ensure cohesion.

When using such a technique care has to be taken that one storyline does not get ahead of the other, that each section should inform the next. Think not of a set of ladder rungs, but of a vertical plank notched alternately on each side. If the notches are cut too close together little headway is made; if cut too far apart it becomes a strain to reach the top.

How would the personnel sound? How would they think? Something that always strikes me as odd when reading futuristic fiction is the way the characters often sound just like we do, using the same syntax, yet if we could travel only 500 years into our past we'd have great difficulty following an overheard conversation. For ease of understanding by the reader, a true rendition of how they might communicate couldn't be used any more than a true rendition of historically accurate speech is used in fiction, but I needed to convey a sense of being outside of our reality.

The back-story included the personnel being descended from

genetically modified humans, and with a history of rebellion against their treatment. Exactly how "human" were they? I wasn't sure, but there again, would they know? I decided that they wouldn't, or wouldn't be sure, thus fuelling a need to reach for what they considered a conspicuous marker of humanity that had been denied them – procreation and nurturing of young.

I've worked in a large industrial organisation where line managers were known by their initials, products by their codes and where department and section titles were truncated. To outsiders conversations could be almost incomprehensible. The same applies to the armed services, as news reports from embedded journalists testify. The emphasis is on speed and ease of understanding within the group. I chose a logical development, keeping sentences short to give a diction slightly off-balance to our ears. I colour-coded the personnel by job to show that the system itself was dehumanising. To add to the effect I termed the planet not by name, but by designation and code. Harvester World TZ29-4.

Once all this background had been established the forward story, the relationships, fell into place. I felt I understood these people, and being able to understand them meant I could become one, for the duration. The unnamed narrator gives a glimpse of her current life while reflecting on snapshots of the past. When something goes seriously wrong in our lives don't we do this, look back trying to work out why we hadn't recognised the impending problem, looking for the moment when, if we'd made an alternative choice, the outcome might have been different?

If making such decisions so as to bring the story to fruition was a complicated process, setting it on the page had to be as simple as possible so as to produce the least resistance in the reader. This is where reader anchorage points came into their own: time, place, focus character, and an intimation of the problem.

The opening short section brings the reader close in to the focus character by using first person viewpoint. The character is injured, yet from the thought processes it would seem there is a larger problem looming, one that had been flagged in the past but ignored. Bringing in a "past" this early was important for the flow between the sections. I also used, without planning to, a phrase that would become keynote throughout the story *Read it as it is and breathe the air*. This phrase would never have risen in my subconscious had I not been in tune with the characters and their setting.

The second section links to the first so easily they could have been a part of a single whole, but that was not my intention. I needed the gap, and for this second section to introduce the "past" and set the place and the time outside the reader's experience, but easily aligned to the SF genre. No one in any day-to-day life stops to consider or describe their mode of dress; parts of it are mentioned only when active. Therefore I used teasers of dress and equipment to give an indication of a work-orientated group, emphasised by the use of the descriptive epithet *Drones* amid the truncated titles of other working groups.

It is established that they are miners, that they are genetically modified beings, that there is cause for concern regarding their treatment, that they are reliant on a life-support system. The conversation marks Mercel as prominent and brings into focus an imminent change to their lives. Again the emphasis is on a problem that readers know from the first section is coming to fruition. The use of the keynote phrase binds the past to the present while the manner in which it is stressed adds weight to the thought processes of the narrator in the first section. The short third section cements the two, setting up the reader to expect this split present-past-present delivery.

If the reader has continued this far, all the background information necessary to make sense of the forward story has been grasped. The reader might not be able to describe either the narrator or Mercel, might not be able to state exactly what they do, but there is enough of an emotional connection for the reader to care so as to want to read on, even though it has been flagged that this dystopian story might have an unsettling ending.

Harvester World TZ29-4. I leave it up to readers to decide what is being harvested, and why. After all, did that white lab mouse understand that it was living merely to grow human ear tissue on its back?

Over To You

Do you recognise your own comfort zone? Do you write only Romance, or only Crime? Do you use only first person viewpoint, or characters of only a certain age or gender? Writers don't extend their skills by continually treading the same path. Dare to try something different.

Conjure a basic premise; write it from a male perspective then write it again from a female perspective. If all you do is change the names and genders then you haven't been paying attention to the commentaries following each story. A character is built from the inside out, depending on that character's experiences and outlook: nature along with nurture.

Write the premise as a Historical, or a Horror, or if you really want to go out on a limb, as Humour. There is no failure, only a learning curve which will inform all your other writing and improve your skills levels.

An Introduction To

Doppelganger

When a writer is receptive, ideas rise up on every side. I'd been speaking to a group of non-writers, trying to dispel the pervasive myth that all fiction is autobiographical, and to explain how characters are generated. I'm not sure they believed me; I'm not sure I believed myself. A bit of musing, and up floated *Doppelganger*.

Doppelganger

If I'd been stone-cold sober I would never have gone up on to the stage.

We were at Kevin's farewell party. He was celebrating; we were drowning our sorrows. I know I was. Kevin's imminent departure meant the title of "Longest Serving Member" was about to be bestowed on me. I'd held it unofficially for months while others, their feet hardly through the dark oak doors, had taken a good look round and found themselves other jobs.

'Lester will never leave. Hasn't got what it takes. He'll still be here when the old man gets carried out feet first.'

I'd overheard that in the cloakroom. The laughter that followed had hurt more than the remark, but the truth of it had haunted me ever since. At my best I was staid; at my worst little more than an automaton, doing the same thing at the same time every single day. Maybe that's why I decided to throw caution to the wind and down every drink that was put before me. By the time the cabaret appeared I'd long since given up looking for reasons and was intent on showing my disparaging colleagues that I did have a more exuberant side to my nature.

The cabaret was a hypnotist. I must have uttered something idiotic, like *It's all fixed*, I can't quite remember, but when a volunteer was called for firm hands wheeled me forward. I remember grinning at the audience, their individual forms lost in the glare of the lights, and I remember the hypnotist speaking to me. The next moment I was having my hand shaken and being led off the stage.

I was disappointed, to say the least. I thought I would have had some recollection of what had happened to me, however vague. I'd done it again. I'd allowed myself to be manipulated – not by the hypnotist, he didn't matter – but by my so-called mates. They knew what had happened, I didn't. The taunts would be never-ending and I dreaded them.

I was halfway down the steps before I became aware of the silence. It was eerie; all those eyes caught on me, yet there wasn't a sound. It wasn't natural. People leave a stage to applause, boos maybe, but never such a silence.

As I reached the floor the hypnotist began speaking over the microphone. His tone was jovial, but his gaze was fixed on my every move and I could feel my skin beginning to crawl. I headed for our table as if it were some sort of sanctuary, but the faces there were as expressionless and as wide-eyed as everywhere else in the room. Andy pushed back his chair so fast I flinched.

'Sit down, Lester. You'll feel much better.' His arm slid protectively round my shoulder as he led me to my chair. Chris jumped up like a jack-in-a-box and began waving his arms about.

'A drink. Get him a drink. He'll feel better after a drink.'

I began to laugh. This wasn't real. 'Aw, come on. Don't mess me about.'

A double scotch was pushed in front of me. I'd no idea whose it was; no one had gone up to the bar.

'Drink it,' Chris insisted. 'You'll feel better.'

'I feel fine.'

I swept the faces round the table. I had never seen them so serious, even in the office with Benstead skulking about. Each appeared to be sober, which I knew definitely wasn't the case.

I laughed again, trying to lighten the atmosphere. 'Don't try that. I know nothing happened up there.'

'*Nothing happened?* You've got to be kidding, Lester!'

'Lester, it was *weird*, believe me.'

Believe them? Against my better judgment I found I was being swayed. 'I don't remember a thing, honest. What happened?'

I was met by a wall of silence. My temper rose. 'You *are*

having me on. Fuck the lot of you!'

'It's no joke,' Andy said. 'It's just that we don't know how to put it, where to start. Chris is right; it was weird. The hypnotist put you under. Hell, you went out like a light. He asked what colour your kegs were – you know the kind of thing these people make you do – but you wouldn't answer him, would have none of it. You kept looking round, out into the wings of the stage, up into the roof.

'When he finally got your attention and asked you to do something, you refused. Point blank. We thought it was all part of the act at first, but the hypnotist got agitated, and then you said you'd had enough or something, and tried to walk off the stage.'

Chris took up the tale. 'Yes, but it was *weird*. I mean, your movements weren't *your* movements. I don't know how to explain it. It was as if it wasn't you.'

I sat there with my mouth gaping, trying hard to be rational about what I was hearing and losing out to the amount of alcohol I'd consumed. 'Was my voice different?'

'It wasn't that the sound of your voice was all that different,' Andy tried to explain, 'it was more the way you spoke. You were so damned positive about everything. I mean, you held that hypnotist in utter contempt. That's not like you at all.'

No, it wasn't like me. I was feeling more sober by the minute and I think it was fear that was doing it. What had happened up on that stage?

'Look,' said Andy, 'we'll get the hypnotist down here and let him explain it to you. That'll put your mind at rest, won't it?'

I didn't know whether it would or not and I sat on tenterhooks until the interval.

Richard Garmaine, hypnotist, shook me warmly by the hand and sat himself beside me.

'How are you feeling, Mr Wardell?'

That question, asked by him of all people, sent shivers down my spine. 'How am I supposed to feel? I thought I felt fine, but I'm not sure any more. They keep telling me weird things happened.'

He was trying to look into my face, into my eyes, I guess, but I kept moving my head, not wanting to hold his gaze.

'Please, Mr Wardell, just let me take a good look at you.'

'Why?' I demanded suspiciously.

He gave a short cough and lowered his voice a little. 'I want to ensure I brought you fully back to consciousness.'

I glared at him, giving him his opportunity without meaning to. 'Christ! Don't you know?'

He nodded and smiled, which didn't reassure me at all. 'You are fine, Mr Wardell, nothing to worry about. But a hypnotist must always be certain with a subject as malleable as you.'

Chris scoffed. 'Malleable? You couldn't do a thing with him.'

'I was referring to the ease with which I could hypnotise him,' Garmaine retorted.

'I was told I went out like a light,' I said.

The hypnotist turned to me, his face bright with another disarming smile. 'I would go as far as to say you succumbed due to your own volition. Do you practice self-hypnosis?'

'Good grief, no. I don't know anything about it.'

'You've never been hypnotised before?'

The man was serious. My blood ran cold.

'What exactly happened up there?' Andy asked. 'You didn't seem to have a lot of control over him.'

The hypnotist shuffled in embarrassment. 'Ah, no. I didn't.'

'Then who the hell did?'

Garmaine raised his face, his expression as innocent as a new-born babe's. 'He did,' he said, pointing at me. 'At least, some part of his inner psyche did.'

'His inner *what?*'

'His inner self. His unconscious self. The face we show to the world isn't the only one we have. Inside a weak man a strong man can be fighting to get out – and vice-versa.'

Every eye turned on me. It was like lying on a hospital bed stark naked with doctors standing over me discussing the intricate workings of my body as if I wasn't there.

'Sounds dubious to me,' Chris snorted.

Garmaine turned to him. 'Dubious? A psychiatrist wouldn't agree with you, neither would a hypno-therapist. There are some who regress their patients back into a past life.'

'Past life? What, like they've been reincarnated? That's rubbish.'

'I read a book about that,' Andy mused. 'It was uncanny.'

'Hey, could that be what happened to Lester? I mean, it reacted so unlike him, it had to be someone else, right?'

I stared at them, my so-called friends. Where had this sudden use of *it* come from? I was me, Lester Wardell. I wasn't an *it*.

'Hey, Lester. You could have been a right tough bastard in your past life. Maybe you had a job with a bit of glamour; a pilot or something.'

'Well, one thing's certain. You wouldn't have been a computerised fucking insurance clerk!'

The laughter ran round the table as it had in the cloakroom months before. Their anxiety, their tension, had left them. The effect of the alcohol was creeping back and I, as usual, was the butt of their jokes.

I tried hard to get back into the swing of things after Garmaine left, but the drink tasted foul. I sat there, my false smile fixed firmly in place, wondering how I could extricate myself from the gathering and not daring to try. I'd hate it, but I'd sit it out. I always did.

Garmaine did a second spot on the stage, recruiting another volunteer, this time from the further side of the room. The man did exactly what Garmaine asked of him and the audience laughed until tears ran down their faces. It made me feel sick just watching it. It could have been me making a fool of myself up on that stage, me the cat-calls and filth-laden hollerings were aimed at. I found myself feeling smugly pleased that I'd been uncontrollable, that I'd made Garmaine look the fool instead of the other way round. He deserved it. The satisfaction I gained from knowing that made the rest of the evening worthwhile.

I couldn't sleep that night. I lay on my bed trying to visualise how I'd acted with Garmaine on that stage. I couldn't. The sheer idea of acting confidently, of speaking my mind – and in front of all those watching people – it was just too much for me to grasp. To hold someone in utter contempt. Christ, I wouldn't know where to start.

Although I had no recollections of what I'd done, I knew exactly what reactions my other self had provoked in my colleagues. For the only time since I'd known them they had been awe-struck. They'd sat up and taken note – of me – and I'd been the one who'd made them. Well, some submerged part of me had.

I thought a lot about that, dwelled on it, in fact. I'd had dreams where I'd been assertive, heroic almost, standing up to bullies, rescuing damsels, being – er – rewarded by them for my efforts. You know the sort of fantasies I mean, but what if they weren't dreams at all, not true dreams? What if it was my other self trying to hammer its way through to my consciousness?

It was a hell of a thought, one I grasped with both hands. If my other self could get through to my consciousness the changes it could make would be beyond description. For a start I'd tell Benstead what he could do with his job, and there would be no more jokes at my expense, either. I'd shut up that loud-mouth, Chris, with one terse rebuff. That would make them look, all right.

It was a thought which took hold. I could be different. Better. All my other self needed was a little help to get through. Even when the alcoholic haze had dissipated and I stared at the reflection of my coated tongue in the bathroom mirror, the idea still seemed sharp. If a hypno-therapist could stop someone smoking, or stuttering, or whatever, one could bring my other self to the fore a little. Why hadn't I thought of this years ago?

Over the next few days I made enquiries and a list of people I thought might be able to help me. It wasn't a long list. Hypno-therapists might seem ten-a-penny in the classifieds but they don't charge pennies. I baulked at some of the fees that were quoted, but I decided that even if it made me bankrupt it would be worth it.

I found one who was fairly reasonable and, in my biggest show of confidence for years, I made an appointment. Which was when I got cold feet.

I hadn't told anyone at the office. I'd had some wild notion that I'd just walk in one day, a changed man; but I needed some reassurance that I was doing the right thing and I had no one outside my work-life that I could talk to. Besides, it might be a good idea to warn them in case they thought I'd flipped and had me carted off to a psychiatric ward.

It took me two days to pluck up the courage to speak to Andy. He was the only one who had ever shown the slightest concern for my feelings. There had been moments, of course, when I could have cheerfully spat blood at him, but of all my colleagues I knew Andy would listen.

He shook his head and moved his weight from one foot to the other. 'I realise what you are trying to do, Lester, I realise what hopes you have, but I don't think it's a good idea.'

I was astounded. I suppose I'd expected him to clap me on the back and tell me it was about time, or something.

'You don't know what you're getting yourself into,' he said. 'You never saw the way you acted under hypnosis. It wasn't just weird, it made my skin crawl.'

I knew what was wrong. Andy didn't want me to change. He liked me the way I was, docile and pliant. Where would he and the others get their fun from if not from me?

'You can't be certain that what we saw was part of your

subconscious. You're just taking it for granted, Lester. I mean, it might have been something else. A past life, for instance.'

'A past life!' I'd thought he was being serious and he was treating this whole conversation as a joke.

'Don't mock it,' Andy retorted. 'I read this book and it damned well unsettled me. I wish I'd still got it. I'd get you to read it.'

Exactly where, I don't know, but somewhere in that short exchange I found the reassurance I needed. I'd show them. I'd show the lot of them.

I stopped by a few shops on the way home, stylish shops, their windows full of the fashionable clothing I'd always avoided. The new me would need new clothes, brighter, better-cut clothes, more in keeping with someone positive and self-assured. Tomorrow was my appointment, the next day Saturday. I'd come back and send my credit card through the roof.

Friday was a hell of a day to work through. I was jittery the whole time. Nervous excitement, I supposed. Andy kept frowning in my direction, but didn't say anything. I was surprised to realise that he hadn't said anything to the others, either. Nobody ribbed me about my appointment. Obviously, nobody else knew. I caught him as we were closing the office.

'Thanks for not telling the others,' I said.

He half nodded, half smiled, and then a grim look crossed his face.

'You've not changed your mind?'

I shook my head and he sighed in resignation. 'Then let me come with you. It'll be good to have a bit of moral support, and besides...' his voice quietened and he licked his lips, 'besides, it might be an idea to have someone on hand you can count on, just in case.'

'In case of what?'

'In case this hypnotist isn't sure whether he's brought you out of it properly. Garmaine wasn't sure, was he?'

'Garmaine was a charlatan.'

'Well, at least I know you. I will be able to tell if something's wrong.'

I thought about it. I could certainly have done with some moral support. 'You promise you won't give the others a blow-by-blow commentary on Monday?'

'Of course I won't. Did I tell them about your appointment?'

I felt quite pepped, waiting for Andy to come off the phone. Even without being my new self it seemed that I had a friend I could trust. It gave me a sense of wellbeing. Today was truly going to be a breakthrough.

The rooms were small but well decorated, the appointments' secretary efficient and welcoming. Dr Harshof was older than I expected, a little doddery in fact. Andy frowned at me, but I ignored him and explained to the doctor why there were two of us.

'Most people like to bring a friend to their first consultation.' He peered at Andy through his glasses. 'If you wouldn't mind taking a seat in the waiting room, young man.'

Andy gave me a quick wink and left. I felt awkward, as if I'd been cast adrift, and it took a determined effort not to walk out after him. Dr Harshof smiled at me and indicated a comfortable chair opposite his own.

'I shall, in fact I am now, recording our conversation,' he pointed to a small microphone on an adjacent table, 'and I shall continue to record all that passes between us until the end of the appointment. A client's problem is rarely ironed out in one session and I find an audio recording a good method of charting progress. The microphone is very powerful and will pick up even the smallest noise, so don't feel that you have to speak into it.'

The doctor settled himself in his chair while I tried to swallow my nerves. If he hadn't mentioned the microphone I doubt I would have noticed it. Ignoring its existence was going to be harder than he maintained.

'Well, Mr Wardell – Lester – we have a lot of talking to do before I can decide whether submitting you to hypnosis will be beneficial. Perhaps you'd like to tell me everything, absolutely everything, to enable me to make an accurate assessment.'

My palms were greasy. In fact, I felt clammy all over, but I forced myself to talk to him, to tell him what I've told you. He was nodding way before I'd finished.

'You wish to be less inhibited, more confident. I understand. Yes, I think it's worth a try. One can never tell until one tries, of course, so I can't promise anything.'

He smiled at me and I forced a smile back. I wasn't sure he did understand. I just wished he'd get on with it.

'Now, remove your jacket and your shoes and make yourself comfortable. I want you as relaxed as possible.'

I tried hard to relax, but I was sweating again and my tongue felt like a sheet of sandpaper.

'Ready?' He dimmed the lights and lifted a hand in front of my face. 'Lester, I want you to focus—'

It was different from the last time. With Garmaine, I hadn't known that I'd even been put under, but on this occasion I did. I was pleased; I would understand what was going on and there'd be no chance of me suffering the resentment I had the last time.

I looked about me, waiting for whatever would happen to happen. Dr Harshof must have dimmed the office more. It was quite dark, not totally black, but too dark to see much – to see anything, really.

Perspiration forced itself through my pores in one fear-filled pulse. *I couldn't see anything.*

I gripped the arms of the chair, but my clawing fingers passed straight through them without a single sensation. I launched myself out of the seat, half admitting, half denying the slow realisation that there wasn't a chair there at all. I turned round to face the space I'd just been sitting in, determined to know the truth. I couldn't see the chair. I felt for it with my hands, but there was nothing there to touch. I stepped back feeling sick – and looked at the floor.

Was there a floor? Standing there, motionless, it felt as if there was a floor. A thick carpet-pile moved beneath my feet. But it shouldn't move, should it, not if I wasn't moving.

I jumped a mile – it seemed like a mile – trying to escape my predatory surroundings. It took a long time for me to float back down again – and I was floating, of that I was sure, floating as if attached to some gigantic parachute.

I touched the floor again. It held me, but I could still feel it moving beneath my feet, a truly odd sensation. I tried to think of it as normal, tried to ignore it, tried to think. I forced myself to be calm. If I wasn't calm I wouldn't be able to do this, and if I didn't try I'd never know.

I stepped off the floor down on to a stair, and then down on to another stair, and then down on to another. And then I cried out. There weren't any stairs; I'd just made myself believe there were. There hadn't been a chair. There wasn't a floor, or a ceiling, a wall, or a building. There wasn't anything. I was in some sort of void where nothing existed.

Did I exist? I forced myself to believe that I existed. The alternative was too horrifying to contemplate.

I exist. I exist. I exist.

I patted my arm with my hand. I patted both arms with both hands. I patted my legs and my chest, pushed my fingers through my hair, felt my face, the slight stubble I'd grown since breakfast. Every part of me was there. I existed.

Thank God.

I looked about me. There was nothing to see. I looked at the darkness itself. There was an opacity about it which shifted in its density.

'Hello?' I said. 'Is there anybody out there?'

My voice sounded hollow, far away, the question positively stupid. I stared into the shifting darkness until my eyes ached with the strain. I hadn't been wrong. Part of the moving darkness wasn't moving. Was something really there, or was that part steady because I wanted to believe it was steady?

'Hello?' My voice sounded tremulous this time, still very hollow, still far away. 'Please answer if you're there. I can't see too well.'

'I'm here.'

I gasped with the shock of hearing an answer.

'Are you all right?'

The voice sounded genuinely concerned and I almost burst into tears. 'Don't go away,' I said. 'I must talk to you. Don't leave.'

'I won't.'

It was a woman. Her voice wasn't particularly soft, rather low-keyed, in fact. She sounded neither young nor old. It didn't really matter. She was someone to talk to, someone who might be able to explain what had happened to me.

I tried to walk towards her, but I wasn't covering any distance. My heart sank. Perhaps she wasn't real, after all. Perhaps I'd wanted someone so desperately that someone had come into existence, just as the stairs had.

I stared at her. She didn't look like a woman, or even a human being. She was just a vague shape, a non-moving piece of the darkness which surrounded me. Emotion exploded in my chest and surged up my throat. 'You don't exist!'

'I do!' Her voice was fierce now. 'I do exist! If you don't want me here just say so. Don't say that I don't exist!'

I bit back my panic and wiped one eye. A hallucination wouldn't speak like that, would it?

'I thought you'd be different,' she continued. Her harsh tone had eased a little. She sounded more hurt than aggressive. 'But you're not, are you? You're just like Lester.'

'I am Lester,' I said. 'I am Lester.'

She didn't reply at once. When she did her voice was quieter still. 'Yes, I know you are. I meant the strong Lester.'

She was talking as if there were two of us. Good God! There

were two of us. She was taking about my other self.

'You mean the other Lester?'

'The strong Lester?'

There was a strange quality about her voice now, which made my skin prickle. It took me a long time to get my tongue round the words I wanted.

'How many Lesters are there?'

'I don't know,' she said. 'Lots. I don't know exactly how many.'

'I – I don't understand.'

She didn't answer. The darkness began to grow oppressive.

'What is this place?'

'Lester.'

Perspiration oozed across my back. I felt as if I were breathing through syrup.

'You mean, we're *inside* Lester?'

'Inside? This is Lester. You are Lester. I am Lester.'

My voice rose an octave. '*You're* Lester?'

'Of course. I'm the feminine Lester as you are the introvert Lester. There is the avaricious Lester and the—'

'No! You don't exist! You don't exist!'

'Don't say that,' she snapped. 'The strong Lester was always saying that, always shouting he didn't belong with us. We thought you'd be different, but you're exactly the same.'

I slapped my hands over my ears, trying to block out her voice. Each sob I expelled hollowed my chest a little more. I fell to my knees in my misery. This wasn't happening. This could not possibly be happening to me.

A sudden draught, as if a door had opened and closed, swirled the silent darkness round me. I held my breath and forced my eyes as wide as I could, desperate to fix on an image.

'Don't leave me!'

I struck out with my arms, flailing the darkness, trying to find where she'd gone, but there was nothing, nothing except the swirling, silent void.

*

'I don't know what to say,' Andy murmured.

I raised my eyes from the rippling thick-pile carpet and rested them on Andy. He was rippling, too, sitting cross-legged opposite me in the gloom. The rippling didn't matter, not really.

'Say nothing,' I said. 'It's just good to have you here.'

He smiled at me. 'That's okay. Things will be different now.'

I nodded and smiled back. It's what I wanted to hear. It's what I'd wanted all along, for things to be different. The rippling I'd get used to. Eventually.

Commentary

The concept I'd been trying to explain to the non-writing group was that although most fiction is anything but autobiographical, the generation of characters, or at least character traits, comes from within the writer.

Humans have a wide range of emotions. Given their head, these can culminate in the sort of dire headlines to be found in any newspaper. That's why society has guidelines for behaviour, why different strata of society have ancillary guidelines, why family groups insist on even more guidelines. Some of these are contradictory, but all exist to bolster an alleged status quo, to keep the mass heading in the same general direction with the least friction.

I perceived Lester as isolated, needy, lacking in confidence, depressed without realising, wanting his life to change for the better but not knowing how to achieve this. Is this me? No, but aspects of that list have been me on occasions during my life, the same as during my life I've been extroverted, opinionated to excess, nurturing, impulsive, studious, loyal, abrasive, persuasive, charming... you get the idea. And this is how we all are, on occasions during our lives.

A writer sets up a character with a proposed set of emotional traits and then trawls back through his or her own experiences to find corresponding incidents, and their emotional resonance, that can be drawn on. If I'd been writing a novel I would have dredged through Lester's early life to discover how he came to be this way, but knowing why wasn't as necessary for the story as knowing that he'd reach for an easy escape.

So how did all this become matched to a trip to a hypnotist? I've never been to see a stage hypnotist, I find the idea somewhat chilling, but I attended a business presentation where a hypno-therapist was explaining states of relaxation. He needed seven volunteers, explaining that people tend to fall into four broad categories. Although I can't recall his actual terms they ranged from the instantly malleable to the highly resistant. I was there to take notes, but he was one short of volunteers and so...

   We sat in a row, closed our eyes and followed his instructions as to our breathing while concentrating on the tone of his voice. And I did feel relaxed, inordinately relaxed, with a marvellous sense of contentment and wellbeing. When he'd completed that initial stage he began to make suggestions: that we should lift our right hands to reach for a balloon, that the balloon was edging out of our reach; that we had a leaden left arm we couldn't drag from the floor... nothing untoward, just enough to show the results to the rest of the group. I, and the other volunteers, were fully aware of the noises in the room, of what was being asked of us, that there was no balloon, that it was ludicrous that we might have a leaden arm. Yet despite this, from the audible reaction of the watching group, it seemed that the other volunteers acquiesced, whereas I was swathed in a warm, relaxing glow and my only thoughts were akin to *go away; I'm comfortable; I'm not moving; don't be stupid.*

   During the discussion afterwards it was unanimously agreed that I – and I alone – fell into the highly resistant category. But why? How was I resistant? Why was I resistant? And more to the point, why weren't the others? What would it have felt like if I'd been a part of the instantly malleable category, knowing that I was following each suggestion as it was given, but being, presumably, unable to stop myself from doing so? I stored the information, and my unanswered questions, until I was seeking story ideas for a Fantasy magazine.

   Doppelganger illustrates the parameters of short fiction: to illuminate a single snapshot of a person's life at a point of change. But note how little back-story, how little description, is placed on the page. In this instance, the use of first person viewpoint mitigates the lack. Lester Wardell is used to his surroundings, so over-used to them that they pale in his consciousness, reflecting the perceived monotone of his life where he believes everyone but him is enjoying a better time, and if he could only be like them he, too, would find fulfilment. Contrast this story to *Shared With The Light*, a story which concentrates on another isolated character, but where there is a depth of description evoked through the filter of the music which fills that character's life.

First person stories dealing with internalisations of the self are often enhanced by the inclusion of secondary characters. Whereas the story opens with a group, only Chris, Kevin and Andy are named, and it is soon established that Andy is the secondary character and the others are merely subsidiaries. Andy is used both as a sounding board and as a goal in the story: someone for Lester to interact with, someone for him to admire. At the very end it is Andy that he conjures as a shade to help maintain his sanity amid myriad different Lesters, each maintaining a pretence of being the only one.

Downbeat, yes, but hopefully thought-provoking.

But, did you believe in the story as it progressed? How about if it was offered as a premise: an insecure young man realises that under hypnosis he has a more vibrant side which he determines to release, inadvertently swapping entities and locking himself inside his mind.

Would you be sold on that proposal?

This is where Structure plays its true part, not just in delivering the storyline in a logical progression, but in carrying readers through steps of explanation so as to help suspend their disbelief. In short, the story isn't rushed. Lester, and in part Andy, voice and then discharge the points of ridicule which should be occurring naturally in readers' minds. This is accomplished via a rollercoaster of viewpoint character emotions.

In order:

hints of being bullied
wanting to break free
disappointment that he couldn't recall stage presence
suspicion at colleagues' reactions
daring to believe
horror at lack of hypnotist's control
hypnosis given credence as a tool of change
colleagues extrapolating outcome
dejection as return to taunting
smugness as witnesses other's ridicule
rationalising possibilities
embraces that the future can be different
spurt of confidence
hint of loneliness
petulance on rebuff
determination in face of warnings
accepting of Andy as supportive
moment of indecision
confidence grows
fear
realisation turns to dread
confusion
dawning of reality
fighting reality
acceptance of and coping with reality

If the points were marked as an extending line graph, positive influences gaining an up-tick, negative influences a downtick, this would certainly be no flat line chart. In part, this is what structure supports, not just the delivery of the storyline progression, but the suspension of disbelief in readers and a manipulation of their emotions.

Did you notice the foreshadowing on p169? *...but I forced myself to talk to him, to tell him what I've told you...*

Who is Lester speaking to? Who is the *you*? Because of the run of the story so far, the initial assumption is that he is speaking directly to the reader. By the end of the story the reader realises that he is speaking to Andy, or at least a virtual rendition of Andy. So why use the foreshadowing?

I wanted to flag that the delivery of the story was not as straightforward as was being suggested. Most fiction has the reader outside the world of the characters voyeuristically looking in. The distance is indicated by the writer's choice of viewpoint – third person inherently carries more distance than first person – as well as the choice made as to the distance itself. As an example, the reader is set closer to this story than the reader is set to *Permanently Portugal*, despite both using third person viewpoint.

Doppelganger explores aspects of reality. By dragging in the reader unexpectedly, if momentarily, it gives the impression that Lester knows an unseen reader is sharing his space. It is designed to make the reader pause so as to realign with the shift. At the end of the story, when it is realised that Lester is speaking not to the reader but to Andy, the reader realigns with another shift in reality – in keeping with the theme of the story.

Foreshadowing was used openly up to the middle of the 20th century, for example *...when she closed the door she had no reason to suspect that...* This blatant authorial interjection is now considered crass, but if handled with more subtlety foreshadowing can still be a potent tool.

A final thought about the story as written: Lester is a person put upon by the world at large: a victim. But how much of this is Lester's perception and how much of it is real? If he had been the sort of person who considered a glass half-full instead of half-empty, would he have made the choices he did?

Over To You

A writer is not an eternal spring of ideas; the well needs to be replenished, and regularly. When did you last experience a stomach-churning, fear-fuelled fairground ride, or stand on a hilltop to drink in the majestic views? When did you last visit an art gallery or a museum? When did you last take a night walk through the country, or close your eyes and listen to the sea talking with the shingle? When did you last do something out of your norm?

Writing is a sensory craft. The actual placing of words onto the page is the final part of the process.

Make a date to do something different. Immerse yourself in whatever experience is chosen. Ask questions, play *what if..?*

Then write.

An Introduction To

A Wind Across The Plains

Practice doesn't just make perfection, it creates proliferation. The more a fiction writer practises the craft, the more workable ideas spring to mind.

The idea for this story came from research for a historical novel set during the North American pioneer era. As triggers often are, it was a bare line in a dry tome mentioning that the prevalence of the wind across the featureless prairie landscape drove many women mad. That conjured an image which stayed with me for some time: full of hope for a better life, a family gives up everything they have to push into an unknown land, only for the support and nurturer to be viciously disabled by, among other factors, the wind.

It was hardly a jolly scenario, but such a luckless woman's perception of the wind intrigued me. Also, how could I put across in words the unremitting intensity of an element of weather that, due to a featureless landscape, would be almost entirely aural? *A Wind Across the Plains* offers one solution.

A Wind Across The Plains

There is always the wind. On the plains it never dies. I'd been forewarned, of course, rumours, but nothing could have readied me for its searing persistence.

It is not a gale. The pamphlets we read at home in Virginia called it a stiff breeze; to tone the skin and cleanse the lungs, it said.

It dries the skin, browns it like a native's, chaps it until it cracks. The stiffened peak of my bonnet keeps off the sun, but it can't keep out the wind, or its grime. The day's privilege is fought for with the tenacity of protecting one's life, the chance for ours to be the lead wagon instead of we eating the others' dust.

The pamphlets made no mention of the dust. They had spoken of waist-high grass swirling and eddying before and aft, of the wagons as ships surging through an ocean of verdant green.

There is no green. The grass is yellowed and brittle, sharp to the touch like corn husks left too long in the field. And that sound, that *flap-flap-flap* of the canvas near my head, as monotonous as the grinding of the earth beneath the wagon's creaking wheels. *Flap-flap-flap*. The canvas can't be stretched tighter. *Flap-flap-flap*. Where else is there to walk, switch in hand to goad the oxen?

I'm not a man. I can't ride point spying the land. I can't take the rifle and roam to hunt the deer. I'm a woman. I can walk behind the stockline, herding lowing milk-cows I can hardly see, coughing up the dust of two hundred hooves or more, or I can walk here, goading the oxen with *flap-flap-flap* constantly in my ears. *Flap-flap-flap* every hour of every day. *Flap-flap-flap* incessantly.

When the day's march is done and the oxen are watered, then begins the hunt for buffalo dung.

I've never seen a buffalo. Not one has crossed our path, but I've scrambled through gorse and thistle, scratched my arms and torn my skirt, promising myself that if I keep looking, if I just keep looking, I'll find that elusive saviour of the evening's meal.

No underbrush to snag the wheels, the pamphlets told, no stands of trees to hide wolf or mountain lion; the open plain rolls on for ever.

There's no wood, either, to feed a fire.

And when the night creeps in from the east and the men have shared a pipe and discussed the journey to come, then we lay in our tent beside the wagon's wheels and there's the *flap-flap-flap* of the canvas cover and the quicker *flappity-flap, flappity-flap* of the tenting above our heads.

Joshua snuggles close. 'Lulls you to sleep,' he says. It's the first thing he's said to me since sun-up that wasn't an instruction.

They've shared a jar as well as a pipe. I can smell the liquor on his breath. I heard them laughing while I was scrubbing the blackened pan with sand. I don't begrudge Joshua his company, his laughter. There are other women, but they all have children or bellies that are swelling. I have the memory of graves back in Virginia. We don't talk much.

I clench my fists, feeling my knuckles sting afresh. His breathing shallows, lengthens. He leaves me alone with the *flappity-flap, flappity-flap* of the tenting above my head and the deeper *flap-flap-flap* of the wagon canvas beyond.

My eyes won't close. I'll not sleep tonight. I didn't sleep last night. I must sleep; the call is 4 am.

Flap-flap-flap. Flappity-flap, flappity-flap.

I must find respite.

Flap-flap-flap.

The moon stares down through the *flappity-flap* tenting.

Flap-flap-flap.
If I listen hard, I can hear the milk-cows lowing, I know I can.
Flap-flap-flap. Flappity-flap, flappity-flap.
There's no canvas there.
Flap-flap-flap.
The night is so bright, the air so clear.
Flappity-flap, flappity-flap.
It isn't far to walk.
Flap-flap-flap.
Joshua will never know, and the posted guard always sleeps, Joshua told me so.
Flap-flap-flap.
Everything is silver.
Flappity-flap, flappity-flap.
I walk like in a dream.
Flap-flap-flap.
Just a little walk; not far at all.
Flap-flap-flap.
Just away from the noise.
Flap-flap-flap.
Just a little way away.
Flap-flap-flap.
Just for an hour or so.
Flap-flap-flap.
Only an hour.
Only an hour.

Only an hour.

Commentary

For once, this story was written from an idea alone, not with the intention of targeting the idea to a market, but that doesn't mean that the process is any less measured.

The choice of a female viewpoint character was easy enough. However, I didn't want the reader to be observing; I wanted the reader to be experiencing. Because I needed the woman to feel besieged and with no one to turn to, by choosing a third person viewpoint I would be inserting a distance between the reader and the character that I didn't want to establish. Instead, first person viewpoint was chosen so as to bring the reader in close to the woman and, by not giving her a name, she and the reader are fused closer still. Keeping dialogue to an absolute minimum – there are a mere four words from Joshua – ensures that the focus remains on the workings of the woman's mind.

I set her mood at the outset and emphasise it by degrees: the shortness of sentences augments the downbeat interpretation of her surroundings. She sees nothing joyful in her day. I wanted to give an impression that she felt cheated but that the sense of injustice had been flattened long ago by the constant repetition and drudgery of her life.

Would she be aware that she was heading for a nervous breakdown? Considering that even now few sufferers recognise the symptoms for what they are, I decided that she'd not recognise them in herself some 150 years ago, and neither would anyone else. All the travellers would be tired due to the arduous conditions of the journey where most walked the 2,000+ miles alongside their wagons. It would only be a matter of the degree.

Her husband I named Joshua for the aural resonance of the word. Names such as Nathaniel or Benjamin didn't carry the same subtext for me, and David or James were far too modern in their connotations. I didn't want Joshua to be too attentive, so they couldn't be newly-weds.

For her to have children would give her a focus outside herself which I also didn't want. There would certainly have been children if they had been married a number of years, but the mortality rate was high, so I twisted the knife some more. Not only had she had children, but they'd died, and she'd been forced to leave both her home and their graves. It would also give her a tendency to shun the company of other women.

This to-ing and fro-ing when building characters is important and should not be curtailed as it is part of making them live on the page.

With the character basics in place, I turned to the landscape. There are available facsimiles of the pamphlets which circulated at the time, both on the eastern seaboard and in Europe advertising the rich lands available in Oregon and California. Some of the claims concerning the journey across the plains are nothing short of criminal to our eyes, and such are emphasised in the journals travellers kept. The discrepancy between the spin and the reality would be ideal to undermine the woman's confidence in the venture. The choice of draught animals was between mule, horse and ox, with the latter often chosen because of cheaper and easier harnessing equipment and the animal's known endurance. To a 21st century reader, the ox would be a slower, ponderous, animal, so it was chosen for its effect on the page.

This left me with the wind. Should I describe its sound using symbolism or metaphor? To use these methods of conveyance on the page would place images in the character's and therefore readers' heads when I wanted nothing to interrupt its constant battering on the woman's mind. Should I use the different sounds made by wind? I had several tries at this but there is a finite number of ways of describing wind travelling at a constant speed and coming into contact with only wagons.

I pictured instead where the woman would be for most of the journey and mentally became her to listen to the sounds she would hear. Over-riding all else would be the constant flap and judder of canvas. It was only when I again failed to come up with enough different words to do the sounds justice that it dawned on me that the repetitive use of the same words would hold far more power in the circumstances. Sometimes the obvious takes time to filter through.

I toyed with italicising the noises and decided to keep it to add visual emphasis on the page. Note the way, towards the end of the story, the narrative fades but the noises remain constant. Wherever the woman walked, and however long she walked for, the noise of wind against canvas would remain constant because she was carrying the sounds in her head. If I had set this out in a continuous stream of a single paragraph it would have deadened the dramatic effect for the reader.

Despite, for me, what is an obvious ending, I have been asked on several occasions 'What happened next?' The answer is that she just kept walking. People did. Despite initial observations, the plains are not flat; they undulate. Without features it was easy to become disorientated, and it was surprisingly common for riders, or children playing on foot, never to be seen again.

Even before I'd completed the story I realised that an ideal market would be radio, but despite interest this never came to fruition. With the march of technology it strikes me that it would work well as a podcast. I need the time to learn how to use the software, so for the moment this idea is on the backburner.

However, it has found favour among poetry audiences, much to my surprise. I shouldn't be so blinkered, and neither should you. Which of your fiction might work better in another medium?

Over To You

Sound is only one of the five senses available to us, the others being sight, smell, taste and touch. Beginner writers tend to over-use sight and ignore the rest, probably due to our living in an age of television and film. Practise using the other four so as to increase skills.

As this story focuses on sound, take the other senses in turn and consider how each might be expressed on the page. Marry this to a character and a situation, and give it a go. A piece of writing doesn't have to be long to be effective.

An Introduction To

Editing

It is all well and good this book giving glimpses of my thought processes as I bring a story from idea to fruition, but a very important step has been ignored – the self-editing. Each story read was not the story written; it was the story polished.

Early in my career a piece of fiction might be rewritten several times until I felt I was conveying the nuances I sought. From brain to hand something was always lost, and it was in the rewriting stages that I picked up those losses, or most of them, and wove them back into the whole.

When I was first published, when my fiction was edited professionally, it was a revelation, and I still have my old copy typescripts painstakingly marked in red to match the published versions. It became my goal, a point of professional honour, to submit a typescript that would match the published version. I wanted my name to be linked to fiction that would require no editing. Time is money, and editors are busy. If they know from experience that a submission from a certain writer needs minimal work on their part, not only does the submission rise to the top of the reading pile, but it will also be chosen over a better story that needs a lot of editing work. Why? Because this is the real world.

When I became a writing tutor, then a fiction consultant, those same initial mistakes I'd made began to pass before my eyes, and it is those mistakes that this section is dedicated to bringing before *your* eyes so that you won't unwittingly do yourself a disservice by passing them on to an editor.

Does your story have conflict?
A short story has to be about something, it has to have a point to it, otherwise it is a study: for example, of a thing – a landscape or a person – or of a state of mind. The fiction might be beautifully written, but where is it going, what is at stake?

Does your story start in the right place?
There is a lot of preamble in a writer's thought processes when conjuring an embryo story, not least in considering a character's past life so as to be able to portray that character true-to-life on the page. You might need to know that your character spent four years in the army, but if this information is not pertinent to the storyline, or pertinent to the character's emotional responses in this story, then to readers it is superfluous information.

The same applies to the ongoing story. Do readers need to follow that character through a broken night's sleep due to gorging on cheese and pickles, through the morning's toilet and breakfast routine, through the trip to work, through saying hello to the receptionist... if the nub of the story is physically centred round the office water cooler?

Beginning at a moment of change, of decision, of minor crisis, helps hook the reader into the fiction. If, in your story, the moment of change, of decision, of crisis, does not erupt until a third, or halfway, through the typescript, you need to ask it why, and what can be cut. Readers, especially editors, will not hang round until the story gets into gear.

Is your story overloaded with description?
Do readers need to be aware of the different types of vegetation growing in every crack in the pavement, or the amount of rust on a beer can in the gutter? Or, indeed, that a character's eyes are *...a striking cornflower-blue...* or *...matched the rich cerulean of the Tasman Sea an hour before nightfall...*? Which character is thinking in these descriptive terms? Often it isn't a

character at all, but the writer supposedly being *writerly*. Description should enhance the story, not *be* the story. What are needed are deft touches filtered through a character's viewpoint, just enough for readers to gain an approximation and so allow them to mentally dress the scene from their life experiences.

If it is necessary in the story for characters to be delineated by their height don't fall back on bald measurements. Have them step up onto a box to reach something that would be handy to most of us, or duck their head as they enter a room; have them be self-conscious or pragmatic about their height, just don't state "the facts" as if writing a police report – or your character notes.

Does your story stay with the chosen viewpoint and distance?

Third person or first person viewpoint makes little difference. Almost everything that is seen or occurs should be filtered through the viewpoint character's thoughts or senses. Omniscient viewpoint is a trap marked "Authorial", and it is all too easy to cross the dividing line. Is this story about your characters or how you feel about your characters? Get off the page and let them do their own thing.

If readers start a story close in to the third person viewpoint character, sharing his every thought, keep to that distance, don't push readers to arm's length during action sequences. If you have difficulty keeping so close in, return to the opening and match the distance to that used later in the story. The flow should be smooth, part of a single whole.

How have you crafted your story's dialogue exchanges?

Speech should enhance the storyline, be in keeping with the characters' backgrounds, the time and physical setting of the story, but it should not be a verbatim rendition of real life. Fiction is a focused construct; real life is organic and self-propelling. In real life we use dialogue to grease the wheels of social intercourse. We don't listen to half of what we hear, our brains continually sifting for phrases pertinent to our individual circumstances. Readers aren't going to wade through that sort of jumble. If you need to portray that sort of jumble – and few stories do – keep dipping into the viewpoint character's thoughts and actions as a method of summarising the information being conveyed.

Are you making the most of dialogue tags?
Dialogue tags are important. Keep them simple and do not augment them with adverbs. *Said* becomes opaque in the run of a conversation, especially when it becomes necessary to delineate who is speaking in an exchange of more than two people.

A dialogue tag also acts as a pause in a string of speech, so take care where it is sited. Replace with action for weight, keeping it short so as not to detract from the spoken words. Readers will take the inference not just from the one line of speech, but in partnership with the narrative that surrounds it. Subtlety in pacing is the key.

'No, I don't think so.'
'No,' said Jerry, 'I don't think so.'
'No,' Jerry said, lifting his gaze to stare at me. 'I don't think so.'
'No,' said Jerry. He lifted his gaze to stare at me. 'I don't think so.'
'No.' Jerry lifted his gaze to stare at me. 'I don't think so.'
Jerry lifted his gaze to stare at me. 'No, I don't think so.'

Have you studied your sentence construction?
Do most of the sentences start with *He / She / It / They*? Are all the sentences the same length? Are you, or is your character, continually summarising? You are writing enthralling fiction, not a dirge – dramatise.

Are you using the correct word?
Is it desperate or disparate? Procrastinate or procreate? Watch your *where*, *were* and *wear*, your *lie*, *lay*, *laid* and *lain*. Would your character *opine* his speech, or *say* it? Would she *grab a cab* or *hail a taxi*?

Are you using the same word in close proximity?
This is down to proofreading skills, of reading and analysing what you have written, not what you think you've written and so expect to see. Words repeated in a rhythm hold a powerful subtext, but not if it is happening elsewhere on the page by accident.

Are you checking for punctuation lapses?
Study a section of any of the stories in this book. If your punctuation doesn't match up in the way it is placed within a sentence or round dialogue, find out why.

Check how many times exclamation marks are used. Once or twice a story is more than enough, certainly not half a dozen times per page.

Check the use of apostrophes. *It's* or *its*? Speak the contraction out fully as *it is*. If the sentence doesn't make sense then an apostrophe is needed. *Diners'* or *diner's*? An apostrophe after the *s* denotes more than one diner; before the *s* denotes a single diner. How many are eating at your table?

When using an apostrophe to denote a missing initial letter in colloquial speech, ensure that apostrophe is facing the correct way ...*t'were 'im, sir*... looks amateurish. ...*t'were 'im, sir*...is how it should be set out. Running the two words together as *were'im* and then inserting a space ensures the apostrophe faces the correct way without resorting to either Symbols or Copy & Paste.

How often are you paragraphing? This isn't just equating to the pacing of the story, but the intended mode of the publishing medium. Paragraphs in printed books can be much longer than paragraphs in a magazine which features three or four columns across the page. An e-reader set to a normal font size might give only 120-150 words to a screen page. Try not to deliver a block of text that fills the screen.

Punctuation matters. Modern production methods mean that a submission is poured digitally into publishing software, whatever the medium. Something as innocuous as extra spaces might mean the difference between acceptance and rejection because it is too labour intensive, ie expensive, to remove them during the editing process.

If you wish to be treated as a professional, be professional. As near as you can, turn in a typescript ready to publish. Is there luck involved in gaining an acceptance? There is always luck involved. The trick is to lower the odds by producing the best fiction you can, no matter the target market.

> Most of all enjoy your writing.

> If you have found this book useful
> please consider leaving a short review
> at your chosen retailer

Other Titles by Linda Acaster

The stories contained in this guide, all written by Linda Acaster, were chosen to highlight specific techniques used in creating short fiction and were selected from over 70 published in genres as disparate as crime, fantasy, SF, women's, historical, romance and horror.

Linda Acaster is an award-winning writer of five novels and a wealth of magazine articles on writing fiction. *Exploring Short Fiction – First Thought To Finished Story* is the first title in the *Reading A Writer's Mind* series.

Other titles include:

Contribution to Mankind and other stories of the Dark
– a short collection of previously published dark fantasy and science fiction stories.
Availability: all-formats ebook.

Reviews: *…from the slightly whimsical "Our Tyke" with its tale of a supernatural friendship no one expected, to the title story about organ-donation and a deadly feud, these are stories which will leave you looking over your shoulder…*

Torc of Moonlight – Book One in a trilogy of paranormal thrillers set in northern England where the past erupts into the present in passion, betrayal and revenge.

For Nick Blaketon university means sex, sport and alcohol with a bit of studying on the side. When he falls for history student, Alice, to win her over he joins in her quest to discover the shrine to a forgotten Celtic water goddess.

Alice has the knowledge, but it is Nick who experiences the visions. At first just uncanny, these soon take on a chilling edge. Someone is in danger, but in the past or in the present? By the time he realizes that he is living a dual life, Alice knows she is in danger and fears Nick is the cause. Can he stop her fleeing to the shrine, or must he face the past on its own blood-soaked terms? Which of them is it truly after?

Heat level: sensual. Availability: paperback & all-formats ebook.

Reviews: *...a fascinating thriller rich in pagan sexuality...in starkly elegant prose, builds a powerful novel of possession and psychological breakdown...a darkly chilling read...*

The Bull At The Gate – Book Two in the *Torc of Moonlight* trilogy.

Nick has moved to York, a walled mediaeval city of crooked half-timbered houses and tight cobbled streets where historical re-enactment groups of Civil War Parliamentarians and Viking longshipmen thrill the tourists. But deep in the crypt of York Minster sit the foundations of an earlier occupation, the Roman fortress of Eboracum that garrisoned both the infamous Ninth Legion and the Sixth Victrix.

As one of Nick's colleagues is reported missing and the police begin to ask awkward questions about previous events, an artefact from the Temple of Mithras appears on his desk. A clever reproduction, or a 1700 year old relic looking as new as if it had been made yesterday?

Availability: paperback & all-formats ebook.

Reviews: *...ratchets up the continuing story beyond expectation.*

Beneath The Shining Mountains – a Native American historical romance set on the northern plains c.1830s.

'Lover? I have no lover. I am chaste. There's not a man alive who can entice me.'

Moon Hawk is playing a dangerous game. Her heart is set on Winter Man, but why would a man with so many lovers want to take a wife? Challenging his virility captures Winter Man's attention, but their tease and spar soon spirals beyond control threatening Moon Hawk and her family with ridicule and shame. Is this Winter Man's intention, or are deeper resentments rising?

From buffalo hunting to horse raiding, this is a story of honour among rival warrior societies and one woman's determination to wed the man of her dreams.

Heat level: sensual. Availability: paperback & all formats ebook.

Reviews: *...vibrant, funny, poignant ...I loved learning about their customs and rich culture...a beautiful love story, realistic and sensual...should be listed with the classics...*

Hostage of the Heart – a mediaeval romantic suspense set on the English-Welsh border in 1066. Rhodri ap Hywel, prince of the Welsh, sweeps down the valley to reclaim by force stolen lands, taking the Saxon Lady Dena as a battle hostage. But who is the more barbaric: a man who protects his people by the strength of his sword-arm or Dena's kinfolk who swear fealty to a canon of falsehoods and refuse to pay her ransom? Betrayed as worthless, can she place her trust, and her life, in the hands of a warrior-knight shielding dark secrets of his own?

Heat level: sweet. Availability: all-formats ebook & mp3 download.

Reviews: *...a page-turner by anyone's standards... an exciting, nail-biting tale, full of high stakes and adventure... a heart-warming romance with a good dose of intrigue...*

Linda Acaster also writes in the Western action genre under the pen name of Tyler Brentmore.

For current information and sample chapters
or to sign up for a newsletter visit:

http://www.lindaacaster.com
http://lindaacaster.blogspot.com